LEADING
Other
THE ^ WAY

HOW TO CHANGE THE CHURCH PLANTING WORLD

JD PEARRING

EXCEL
LEADERSHIP NETWORK

What people are saying about
LEADING THE OTHER WAY

JD Pearring has hit it out of the park with *Leading the Other Way*! It is a great read, it presents a more successful path to effective church planting, and it is filled with helpful illustrations, quotes, and stories. It inspired me to look at church planting in a different way and convicted me on some false ideas that I have held onto for a long time. If we took his ideas to heart, it would change the trajectory of Christianity in the United States!

Glenn Gunderson, Lead Pastor,
Purpose Church, Pomona, California

Imagine! Just imagine if new churches were led by Holy Spirit-empowered leaders and teams - as described in Acts. And imagine if Christ-followers took seriously JD Pearring's superb color-commentary on how to change the church planting world. *Leading the Other Way* is a discerning and paradigm-changing must-read. Plus, it's laugh-out-loud funny! I mean, when's the last time you enjoyed wisdom from Spurgeon, Mother Teresa, Pogo, and Casey Stengel - all in the same book? Here's my offer: Read the first fifty pages of *Leading the Other Way* - and if you're not deeply convicted about God's plan for the local church and/or you don't laugh out loud at the hilarious stories and humor - I'll send you a Starbucks card.

John Pearson, author, Mastering the Management Buckets

I smiled all the way through reading this book. JD communicated how to change the way we do church planting with great humor. It will be hard to find a book that is both more challenging and encouraging. It is worth your time to read and to pass on to those who care about church planting. Thanks JD for your heart for the lost.

Jack Hamilton, Executive Pastor, High Desert Church

This book is a must read for church planters and leaders working with them. It is an excellent, fun read that is filled with JD's wisdom accumulated over decades of planting churches and serving church planters. JD is a leader that has proven courage, wisdom, and love for the church of Jesus. Buy copies for every planter and pastor you know!

David Houston, Director of ABC3 Church Planting,
Every Nation Churches and Ministries.

Leading the Other Way does more than is promised. I expected the book to provide a practical philosophy for starting churches benefiting church planters, churches, denominational executives, and network leaders. I received even more. *LTOW* gave me insight into the Scripture, my own life, how to lead a church, and how to develop leaders in my business. This book is the cornerstone for my coaching of both church planters and those desiring to take their spiritual leadership to a much greater level. Applying these principles has enhanced both my personal growth and my organization's development. *LTOW* is an indispensable part of my library because of its impact on my thinking and leadership.

David Bennett, Financial Coach, Church Consultant

Some people just know what they are talking about and know what they are doing. JD Pearring is one of those leaders. He brings the credibility of an effective Church Planter and the wisdom of seeing it attempted in every conceivable manner. *Leading the Other Way* presents a thoroughly Biblical and principle-centered – not program centered – approach to planting effective churches which focuses on the leader whom God has gifted and called. I've personally experienced this approach as a pastor of a church which planted churches, and now through leading a national Association committed to planting effective churches.

Dr. William C. Nolte,
Mission Lead at Transformation Ministries

JD is the guru of church planting on planet Earth! JD not only helped our church plant be successful many years ago, he has also helped our church family be healthy. His wisdom has been instrumental for us to plant thriving churches. This book captures much of what JD lives and breaths for church planters!

Brad Brucker, President of Epic Global Missions &
author of GROW: Journey to A Transformed Life

Leading the Other Way is inspired, fun, and intriguing, but as one who has engaged the church planting world for thirty-five years, it brought tears to my eyes as I was convicted of some of the leadership mistakes I still make. I don't know of any other book penned for the same audience, and I am personally grateful to JD Pearring for writing it.

Dr. Linda Bergquist, Church Planting Catalyst,
North American Mission Board

There is no one I know who has invested more and has more experience in every aspect of church planting than JD Pearring. He has been a friend, a mentor, and a leader to me in my church planting leadership. This book is filled with practical, down-to-earth Biblical advice about church planting, leadership, and spiritual health. The stories alone make it worth reading. The church planting world is full of hype, but I know firsthand that JD is practicing what he preaches about partnership, networking, and supporting church planters. I recommend the book, but most importantly, I highly recommend the author!

Josh Wroten, Director of Church Planting,
NextGen Churches

Written with the clear authenticity of a practitioner, JD Pearring's book *Leading the Other Way* takes the essential next steps deeper into the field of church planting. He challenges us to take responsibility for what is, and embrace change for what can be."

Dr. Robert E. Logan

JD Pearring spun me around once before, and now he's doing it again. The first time was after a seminary chapel service devoted to church planting. JD grabbed me and said, "Tom, you have to do this!" So I did. Three decades later, he's still turning me around, saying, "We can do better than this!" *Leading the Other Way* is an outstanding book for those of us concerned about the church planting universe. With a truckload of experience, thought, illustration, provocation, and passion, JD spins us around to a better way to lead. I love what it is doing to me and to us.

Dr. Tom Nebel, Church Planting Guru &
Senior Associate, Giant Worldwide

If you care deeply about the future of the church, not only new churches, but the church as a whole, JD's book will encourage you, irritate you in a healthy way, and motivate you to lead for change. With honesty, authority, and intensity, JD coaches leaders of churches, ministries, and denominations to consider the Kingdom over their respective domains, challenging us to lead for the sake of others. Rooted in Scripture, Pearring's book resonates deeply and should reverberate out widely. He asks tough questions and provides tangible answers via transferable principles, not prescriptions, as only an experienced practitioner can. Read this book if you care more about the church than yourself and you will help both.

Nathan Hawkins, West Regional Executive, Stadia

What I love about *Leading the Other Way* is JD calls us to recover the mission of the Church without sacrificing our soul on the altar of church planting. JD isn't just a thought leader in church planting, he is a church planter. He has been where so many church planters want to go. We can learn from his wisdom. We can be inspired by his passion. We can avoid his mistakes. We can be change agents in the way churches are planted. Healthy, growing churches are the fruit of this book.

Justin Davis, Author of Beyond Ordinary,
Church Planter/Pastor of Hope City Church

The typical church planting book is full of "how-to" information. But there are few church planting books written that are the final chapter that underlines what church planting is all about. Because of JD's experience working with multiple networks and denominations, he's extracted the best bottom-line information and wisdom and passed it down to us in *Leading the Other Way*. A must read for anyone who has anything to do with church planting.

Gary Chupik, National Church Planting Catalyst,
Apostolic Church of Canada

When it comes to church planting, the stakes are high. For too long, we've ignored the issues that plague church planting movements and church planters. If you're open to seeing church planting in a different light then *Leading the Other Way* is a book you will want to read.

Jeff Sharp, Executive Pastor and Church Planting Director,
Rivers Crossing Community Church

JD has done the denominational leader, the pastor, and the planter a kindness by writing a book that kicks us out of our collusion with mediocrity in church planting, calls us to a better way, and humbly lights a path forward. I've been helped by his honest passion for planting and leading, and I believe you will be helped, too!

Adam Mabry, Pastor of Aletheia Church, Boston

I've seen the impact of this message over and over as it inspires and liberates church planters from unnecessary pitfalls in launching new churches. JD Pearring has given us a timely and powerful gift of Kingdom insight and wisdom. If you desire to plant a church or join a church planting movement this is a must read.

Paul Mints, Lead Pastor,
The Community at Lake Ridge, Mansfield TX

Leading the Other Way
by JD Pearring

Published in
collaboration with

LAMP POST inc.
www.lamppostpublishers.com

Published by:

EXCEL LEADERSHIP PUBLISHING

8737 Santa Ridge Circle • Elk Grove • CA • 95624
www.excelleadershipnetwork.com

Trade Paperback: ISBN-13 # 978-1-60039-025-8
ebook: ISBN-13 # 978-1-60039-094-4

To Lori

Contents

Foreword

I first met JD Pearring at Green Lake Conference Center in Wisconsin. I was there leading a Transitions conference. He was there leading a church planter assessment. Since we both had two decades of church planting experience at that point in our lives, we hit it off. When you love the same thing someone else loves, it clicks!

For the past fifteen years, I have watched God use JD in amazing ways. There are a lot of people out there who love church planting. JD is one of them. But he is much more than that.

JD loves church planters! He loves the guys that are leading the charge. He loves the church planter that is scraping out an existence, pouring his soul into the birth of a new church, and laying it all on the line to do so.

Where does this love come from? First – JD is a church planter, so he gets it. Second – JD is a father, and a father is what he becomes to his church planters. Third – God just has His hand on JD. It really is a God thing.

So if you are a church planter, or a pastor who wants to help plant a church, or a Christ follower who is or wants to be part of a church plant, you need to read this book with the right mindset. This is not just a "how to" book from a "how to" guy, although it is that for sure. This is not just a "what do I do when I get stuck" book, although it is that as well. This is a book from someone who loves church planters, who champions church planters, who parents church planters.

Read this book as a gift from God who is lovingly trying to save you a lot of heartache and lead you to a lot of blessing. Because that is what it is!

Dan Southerland, Lead Teaching Pastor
Church Planter Coach
Kansas City, Kansas

Introduction

Six family members were sitting at the round restaurant table, almost finished with a very pleasant lunch, when my brother-in-law raised the issue, "Do we need to talk about what is going on with...you know?" The elephant in the room had been mentioned.

I immediately jumped in, grateful someone else brought up the subject so I wouldn't always be the bad guy. "I do need to say something," I stated. "I just want you to know that I am so very sorry that this latest round of antics has happened to you. It isn't right, you didn't in any way deserve this, and it is simply awful." My emotions caught me, then I added, "I want you to know that I am available to help financially or otherwise as you – as we – deal with this."

"It's been going on too long, and now this... This is the worst," someone said.

"Why don't we just give him more money?" another family member proposed.

Several voices responded in unison, "We already tried that and it is still going on."

"Money doesn't heal hearts," one quipped.

"I just want the abuse to stop!" someone else muttered.

"Let's stop enabling…"

"But what about compassion? He can't help it, he didn't really have a father…"

"It may not be all his fault, but when will he take responsibility?"

My wife Lori, the counselor, spoke up. "Some of us here are primarily thinkers, and others of us are mostly feelers. That's why we look at this problem differently."

"But if we keep on doing the same things and expect a different result…" I started.

"That's insanity!" one of my relatives shouted.

"It's at least silly," I mumbled. "But we have to admit, what we have been doing hasn't worked, otherwise we wouldn't be here, dealing with this."

"One of the issues," my brother-in-law conceded, "is we've all been trying to deal with this differently. We need to get on – and stay on – the same page."

This book, like that family situation, is a challenging, awkward, difficult conversation.

The elephant in the room is the way we have been planting churches in the United States and North America. Church planting hasn't been working as well as it could, as well as it should, or as well as we all have hoped it would. We need to admit there is some dysfunctionality going on. I'd rather not be the bad guy and bring up the issue, but it has been going on too long. I've been planting churches, working with denominations and networks, and helping others plant churches for thirty-plus years – I've been in this church planting family for a long time – and not only am I sorry that some things have gone wrong, I am sorry for my part in the dysfunction, and I am here and available to see things get turned back around.

Can we talk about this? Can we address some of our harmful antics? Can the abuse please stop? Can we admit that if we keep doing things the way we have been doing things, we are silly, if not crazy, to think we will see big changes?

I would love for us to get on the same page. That page is page 1668 of my study Bible, specifically Acts 13:

> In the church at Antioch there were prophets and teachers: Barnabas, Simeon called Niger, Lucius of Cyrene, Manaen (who had been brought up with Herod the tetrarch) and Saul. While they were worshiping the Lord and fasting, the Holy Spirit said, 'Set apart for me Barnabas and Saul for the work to which I have called them.' So after they had fasted and prayed, they placed their hands on them and sent them off.
>
> —Acts 13:1-3

I would like us to get back to Acts 13, to get back to the book of Acts, to the Bible, to be working from the same set of blueprints. I am ready to help us change the church planting world, and I think we can.

By "we" I mean the groups of people mentioned in that passage: Church planters, church planting team members, church leaders who are looking to reproduce their ministry or at least open to planting other churches, plus leaders of denominations and sending agencies with a heart for planting.

This is a challenging conversation because to change means we need to admit we *need* change, it means we need to admit we haven't been on the same page, and it means we need to do the work, and give the arduous effort that change requires.

I don't pretend to have all the answers. I have lots of opinions and even more questions, but I am committed to finding some solutions together.

I am also committed financially to see the church planting world changed. All of the proceeds from this work will go into church planting: half will go for Discovery Center scholarships, to help those who are considering starting a church as their next step in ministry. The other half will go to support church planters as matching funds for their new church endeavors.

This book is set up rather simply:

Part One deals with the *what* and *why* of the issue, along with *who* needs to be involved. Part Two takes a more in-depth look of *how* to get back to the same page from here – the pages of the book of Acts. And Part Three deals with *where* we go from here and *when*.

After each chapter there is a Key Question – I do have more questions than answers! – then there is a "Big Challenge." My current pastor, Tim Pearring, who also is my son, moved our church teaching team away from "The Big Idea" to "The Big Challenge." He suggested we move people to action, not just ideas.

Together we can change the church planting world. Let's embrace, and even enjoy, the journey together.

LEADING THE OTHER WAY

WE HAVE A PROBLEM

Today's problems come from yesterday's solutions.

Peter Senge

It's so much easier to suggest solutions when you don't know too much about the problem.

Malcolm Forbes

We have enough people who tell it like it is. Now we could use a few who can tell it like it can be.

Robert Orben

CHAPTER ONE

MORE THAN BOB

Never doubt that a small group of thoughtful citizens can change the world. Indeed, it is the only thing that ever has.

—Margaret Mead

I alone can't change the world, but I can cast a stone across the waters to create many ripples.

—Mother Teresa.

No crime is so great as daring to excel.

—Winston Churchill

Bob proudly steered his brand new 1984 Honda Accord over Monument Hill from Denver to Colorado Springs while I rode shotgun and peppered him with questions. Bob served as my denomination's executive pastor for our Rocky Mountain region. A former church planter, now he was my boss, church planting coach, ministry consultant, and a kind of grandfather figure. Our church had just entered into our second year of existence, and I was full of ideas and possibilities. Should we go to two services? What about this strategy to make year two even better than year one? How can we help the church planter who we just sent off after interning with our church?

As Bob responded to my barrage of questions, I noticed his answers all sounded the same:

"Give it a shot."

"Go for it."

"Why not try that?"

Suddenly it hit me: *I'm a Guinea pig.* I was an experiment. Our church had already grown larger than Bob's church plant, so he really didn't have many answers. I will never forget the eerie thought that washed over me: "I need more than Bob."

That incident sparked a vision inside of me that I've been pursuing ever since. Can we put together some sort of network where church planters and leaders can learn from those a step or two ahead of them, and bring future leaders and planters to learn from those a step or two ahead of them?

At first, I expected to see these changes take place through my denomination. I jumped on the church planting committee and did what I could to encourage planters and leaders. But the denomination seemed to be more concerned with planting *lots* of churches than planting *effective* churches. We sent out folks who were clearly not wired as entrepreneurs, not relationally inclined, or not gifted leaders. It seemed we were setting some people up for failure.

> **Suddenly it hit me:**
> **I'm a Guinea pig.**
> **I was an experiment.**

Failure as a church planter is especially troubling. You can step into the pastorate of an existing church, run it right into the ground and shamelessly blame the former pastor with, "It was in terrible shape when I got here." Just about everyone will buy that. You can go on to the mission field, spend decades with very little influence, and blame the culture with, "It wasn't fertile ground." Just about everyone will side with you. But if you start a church and it doesn't succeed, it is all your fault. Even God seems to say, "Hey, don't look at me, you're the one who messed it up!"

There had to be a better way. So when I was invited to a church planter assessment center by another denomination, I jumped at the chance. The group put my wife and me through a rigorous evaluation to ensure we were church planters. We went into the event without much anxiety. We'd already planted an effective church. If they told us we couldn't do it, we'd think, "Hey, that's pretty amazing that we did something we couldn't do!" It turned out to be a terrific experience. We learned a lot about intentionality, about how we work together as a couple, and we were reminded of the tremendous need for support as planters.

It was incredibly exciting to be called by that group to start a church in the San Francisco Bay Area. So we moved from Colorado to Northern California and launched our second plant. The new church got off to a nice start, and I was anticipating working with a group that wanted to support planters. I immediately became involved in their assessment process. I started coaching other planters. But I sensed more was needed. Assessment was great, coaching was okay, but where was the network *support*?

Many denominations have developed a pattern of over-promising and under-delivering.

As our new church took off, the new denomination took away their promised financial assistance. "You guys don't need it. We'll use it to start more churches," they reasoned. "But you promised!" I protested childishly. I recognized that denominational leaders have a lot to juggle.

I didn't want this sort of judicatory jerkery to keep happening to church planters.

For them, moving funds from one group to another is just another decision. But to have funding cut off can be devastating for a planter. I was annoyed and angry. We had based some longer-term goals on that pledged funding. I realized that the lack of capital would hamstring our brand new church for a while, but we'd make it.

It is frustrating to be on the front lines of ministry without much financial, emotional and spiritual support, but it is even more frustrating to be on the front lines without support when you were promised support.

I began to recognize that many denominations have developed a pattern of over-promising and under-delivering. My wife graciously calls this, "A big heart and a small memory." Again, the goal of denominations can slip into trying to start a lot of churches, not necessarily thriving ones.

The experience of lacking support a second time was part of a clarification of my passion. I eventually discovered that my passion was not for church planting. My passion is for church planters and leaders.

A few years later, I sensed a call from God to move from the Bay Area and plant a church in the Sacramento area. We would be better positioned to see more new churches start from the state capital region. So I worked out a financial support arrangement with the current denomination.

This time I got it in writing: fool me once, shame on you; fool me twice, shame on me. But the very night we told our church of our plans to move and committed to a hand-off situation for the next pastor, I received a phone call from my denomination supervisor. "You know all that stuff we agreed to about your support?" he asked. "Well, we're not going to be able to do it."

This time I wasn't as much angry or frustrated as I was determined. I didn't want this sort of judicatory jerkery to keep happening to church planters.

I had joined with a few others to see if we could form a support network for planters. It appeared to work. We were seeing new churches start all over the United States. We were putting together systems and events that helped them. We were on the verge of seeing a dynamic organization happen. But a funny thing happened on the way to our vision. The denomination squelched it.

The denominational powers called church planters and leaders to a meeting in Phoenix, Arizona. About fifty church planters came. We waited for the big news from headquarters. They sent one representative – a third-string associate from the finance department. (I know that sounds derogatory, but it's the nicest way I can think of putting it!) This accountant had two simple messages: "First, the denomination is not going to fund this church planting network anymore." (Actually, they weren't putting much money into planting anyway.) "Second, what you are doing is working, so we want you to do whatever you are doing to the established churches so we can save the denomination."

It was a ridiculous message, delivered in an absurd manner by an unsuitable non-leader, who was not competent to answer any of our questions because, well, he was the third-string bean counter.

Immediately we all thought we'd simply leave the denomination and go out on our own. The decision was a no-brainer. But the leader of our church planting group, the one who was paid by the denomination and the only one with an actual vote, spoke up. "This is my tribe. Let's go along and see if we can't save the denomination," he responded. And so the fledgling network was stopped in its tracks.

That was just another one of the incidents that led me to step out of denominational politics. I poured myself into assessing planters, and we grew our church planter assessment center into an entity that serviced over thirty different denominations. I did some coaching and tried to encourage planters when I could. But the network idea seemed dead.

A few years later, I was approached by still another judicatory and asked to lead their church planting efforts. "I'm sorry, I don't do denominationalism," was my reply. They laughed. "Read my book," the director encouraged. "We don't do denominational politics either. We're a region of a mainline denomination, but our stance is we ignore them. My job is to keep them from messing up our region."

I joined the team, and the regional director allowed me to put together a network of planters and leaders. And it took off. We started over a hundred churches in just a few years. We saw planters helping planters, leaders mentoring leaders, and a strong sense of momentum.

During this time, I was approached by a number of denominations and church planting groups who asked if we could help them start churches. At first I tried to do that through the current mainline denomination. Maybe these other groups could come under my present organization, I thought. But that proved way too cumbersome.

I also noticed that our present judicatory was actually becoming a lid on the planting ministry. They had financial issues, structural issues, and denominational issues that made partnering awkward.

I kept banging my head against the ceiling trying to advance church planting under a structural cap. Maybe through all that head banging something broke loose, because an idea popped into my mind. What if we started a sort of phantom organization where we could serve several groups at the same time? As a *Seinfeld* fan, I thought of when George Costanza and Jerry Seinfeld wanted to make up a business, they called it, "Vandelay Industries." What if we started Vandelay Ministries? We did! We started the Vandelay Network. (We later changed the name to "Excel Leadership Network" because it became burdensome to continually explain the *Seinfeld* reference. We've learned that if you have to explain your name, it's probably not a great name!) The idea included serving different organizations and denominations with effective church planting

> I wasn't going to sacrifice the vision again. God had begun a good work and we were going to see it to completion.

systems and environments, while allowing them to keep the unique distinctiveness of their tribe.

I talked the scheme over with the director of the mainline denomination I was working for, and he was on board. His goal was kingdom expansion, and he saw this as one step toward that.

We started helping other groups, and other denominations – mostly evangelical organizations – and the vision was working.

When my mainline denomination director approached retirement, I let him know very clearly that I would follow him and be loyal to him. But if the next regional director didn't want to do church planting, I wasn't going to sacrifice the vision again. God had begun a good work and we were going to see it to completion.

The regional leader retired and a new judicatory director was named. Five days later, the director's wife left him. He was a mess, and so was his divorce. In the midst of this madness he made some questionable hires, strange decisions, and disastrous moves. He also inexplicably turned away from church planting, and turned toward denominationalism. It made no sense and was certain to debilitate the region. I'm not going to go into detail here, this isn't a "tell-all" book, it's not even a "tell-some" book! I think of Gordon Gekko, the Michael Douglas character from the Wall Street movies. In *Wall Street: Money Never Sleeps*, Gekko remarked: "Stop telling lies about me and I'll stop telling the truth about you."

In a heart-breaking, gut-wrenching-but-crystal-clear decision, I left that mainline group. But the vision didn't leave me. Essentially we fired our top customer, but we had other partners, like Transformation Ministries, and amazingly we were able to plant more churches in each of our first two years on our own, than we had with the mainline group. Excel Leadership Network met all of our five year goals in the first eighteen months. We began to fulfill the vision to put together a network of church planters and leaders who will learn from each other, help new leaders, and promote a movement of reproduction in Jesus' church.

We at Excel Leadership Network are targeting church planters, church planting teams, mother churches, and sending agencies to come together, connect, and build a leadership network.

We may not change the world, but we have a very clear BHAG (Big Hairy Audacious Goal), and that is to change the church planting world. We want to change the way church planting is done in North America. And we can.

THE KEY QUESTION:

Who or what may be putting a lid on your current vision?

THE BIG CHALLENGE:

Be diligent to keep the next promise you make.
Refuse to over-promise and under-deliver.

CHAPTER TWO

OUR OWN WORST ENEMY

We have met the enemy and he is us.

—Pogo

The important thing to remember about the phenomenon of sabotage is that it is a systemic part of leadership - part and parcel of the leadership process. Another way of putting this is that a leader can never assume success because he or she has brought about a change. It is only after having first brought about a change and then subsequently endured the resultant sabotage that the leader can feel truly successful.

—Edwin Friedman, A Failure of Nerve

Sabotage is natural. It's normal. It's part and parcel of the systemic process of leadership . . . Saboteurs are usually doing nothing but unconsciously supporting the status quo. They are protecting the system and keeping it in place.

—Tod Bolsinger, Canoeing the Mountains:
Christian Leadership in Uncharted Territory

Twenty-five years ago my wife, Lori, and I were invited to start a church in the San Francisco Bay Area. A friend of mine, let's call him Elliot, was also called to plant a church in the Bay Area at the same time. We lived and served about fifteen miles apart. Elliot and I went through an Assessment Center together, we went through several trainings together, we were even on the same fund-raising circuit together, we ate meals and traveled to meetings together. We were friends and colleagues.

A couple years into our plants, Elliot and I had lunch at a restaurant in between our churches – it was a regular occurrence for us. I asked how things were going, and Elliot replied, "It's not going very well."

So I put on my strategic cap and started in, "Have you tried this? Have you thought of that? We did this and it worked…"

Elliot interrupted me. "My wife isn't coming to church anymore," he confessed.

"What was that?" I asked.

"My wife doesn't come to church, she stopped a couple months ago." I wasn't an experienced church consultant, but I knew that wasn't good. When your spouse stops attending the church you pastor, there's a problem.

I felt there had to be a better way, another way, a different way.

So I stopped talking and let Elliot vent. "I never wanted to do this," he admitted. "The denomination felt they needed some black planters, so we were pushed into this – all of us who were pushed into planting have failed." Elliot went on for a while, and then he said something I will never forget: "Church planting has exploited all my weaknesses, and minimized all my strengths."

Elliot appeared exhausted, defeated, and exasperated as he expressed his discouragement. And I felt there had to be a better way, another way, a different way.

Unfortunately, Elliot's story of being set up for failure in planting a church is not an isolated one.

Andy, a worship pastor at a medium-sized Midwestern congregation began to sense a call to start a church. So he went to his senior pastor with the thought. "Not now," the pastor said. A year later, Andy was still wrestling with the idea, so he went to his senior leader again and said, "I think I might want to start a church." "Not now," the pastor emphasized, "and if you ever do plant, you will have to make sure you move it at least thirty miles from this church!" Another year passed, this time Andy went to his pastor and said, "I think now is the time." So the pastor concluded, "You're fired."

> Andy went to his pastor and said, "I think now is the time." So the pastor concluded, "You're fired."

I wish that scenario was uncommon. Regrettably, fighting against church planting is a typical response in North America.

Jeff was planning on starting a church in Southern California, so his denominational executive took him to meet the pastor of old First Church in the town Jeff was targeting. The pastor of old First Church started in, "Just so you know, we didn't ask you to come here. We're not going to give you any money, we're not going to give you any people, and we're

> Regrettably, fighting against church planting is a typical response in North America.

not happy you are coming here." Jeff thought, "Nice to meet you too!"

Another pastor in the area sent this note to Jeff: "To be clear... We do not have a heart for church plants, and to be quite frank, will not work with church plants."

Stu was brought on to a large church with the clear plan to step out and plant a daughter church. But when the time came and Stu was publicly "sent out," privately he, his family, and his team were exiled. No money, no relationship, no people who were promised ever came through.

Jay took the position of pastor at an older congregation in the San Francisco Bay Area with the stated goal that he would start a new congregation in the evening in the older church's building. Everyone was on board – until the time came for the new church's first service. The leadership group in that church held a secret meeting, then reported to Jay that not only was he not allowed to plant in that building, but he needed to start dressing better and from now on was only allowed to preach from the King James version of the Bible.

Matt tells his story: "From the first day I was hired at a local church plant to lead worship I was encouraged to think about planting a church myself. Every time we'd go to a conference or hear someone's story of planting, the challenge would be raised. After serving in that church for six years, my wife and I gave in to the calling to plant a church, and with the staff and board's blessing, attended a network assessment center. After passing through that assessment we returned back to our local church to tell them of our plan to transition over the coming months to plant a new church. That afternoon, less than twenty-four hours after returning home, I was asked for a list of any passwords I had made on our church server, a current list of projects I was working on, and released from my staff position. This dream I had of planting with my church family and close friends came crashing down and left me unemployed and hindered our planting story for the next four years."

Ivan felt he had put off for too long his call to start a Spanish-speaking church in Southern California. So Ivan told his pastor that he was going to plant a church. His pastor replied, "You will fail. You will come to me asking forgiveness for leaving. You will never plant a church." Ivan's church is now much stronger, larger, and influential than his former pastor's church, but those words still carry a bit of a sting for him.

Brian wanted to move back to San Jose to start a church in his hometown. We arranged funding from several entities, most notably a small denomination that appeared to want to embrace church planting. But one of their churches in Santa Cruz (over a mountain range and over thirty miles away) nixed the project because they feared the competition. That church's average attendance was seven people.

Chris was invited to move from the Northwest to Arizona to start a church launched through the ministry of a pastor friend. So Chris moved his family south. But when he arrived, his friend told him he was leaving to go to California. And the church that was going to launch a new work pulled the plug. Chris was left in a new place with no job and no plan.

When Lori and I started our third church a local pastor told me that they would support our efforts. "What does that look like?" I asked. "I'm not sure," the pastor thought. "It could mean anything from giving you money and people to simply sending flowers for your grand opening. I'll think about it and let you know." A couple weeks later, the associate pastor from that church called an emergency meeting with me. Then, with his senior pastor watching, he proceeded to lay into me about how I was stealing people from their church, and how I had betrayed them. After twenty minutes of listening to his low-level venting, I simply asked, "What are you talking about?" "I just heard that one couple from our church is going to go and help you!" he stated. "That is news to me," I responded, "I had no idea." He calmed down, but it was obvious they were not going to support us. We never got any flowers either.

Church planting in North America has not been as effective as it could be, and we can easily blame ourselves.

It appears that well-meaning, wonderful Christian leaders, pastors, and churches often are the biggest road-blocks to planting more churches.

Panting and perspiring, two men on a tandem bicycle at last got to the top of a steep hill.

"That was a stiff climb," said the first man.

"It certainly was," replied the second man. "And if I hadn't kept the brake on, we would have slid down backward."

It seems that many who we thought or hoped were helping us, may have been hindering us all along.

Years ago, in the National Hockey League playoffs, Barry Beck, a defenseman on the New York Rangers started an ugly brawl that ended up including most of both team's benches. After the game, Beck uttered an infamous quote about the incident. He said, "We have only one person to blame, and that's each other."

Church planting in North America has not been as effective as it could be, and we can easily blame ourselves. Let's stop blaming, and start changing.

Edwards Deming said, "Your system is perfectly designed to get the results you are getting." The church planting system we have in America is perfectly designed to make it difficult for planters to plant.

Ben, a Midwest church planter who had just been messed over by a sending church and his denomination admitted, "It was unintentional, but not unavoidable."

Things must change. I saw this quip recently: "Hamburger Helper: It works, but only if the hamburger is ready to accept the fact that it needs help." We need to admit we need help; we need to change.

Garret was part of a denomination with a culture of firing any church staff person who decided to plant a church. He called me moments before his dreaded meeting with his senior pastor, simply for moral support. We prayed. After the meeting he called me again. "How did it go?" I asked. "I'm stunned," he

> **Hamburger Helper: It works, but only if the hamburger is ready to accept the fact that it needs help.**

said. "The pastor said I can stay on until I am ready to plant, plus they will pay my first year's salary."

Maybe Garret's story is the exception that proves the rule? Why can't Garret's story be the rule?

A few weeks ago I shared some of these stories in a Sunday message. One new believer in his late thirties, a middle-class, hard-working everyman came up to me. "JD, can I ask you a question? Why would churches and pastors fire someone for wanting to plant a church? That doesn't make any sense to me. Aren't we supposed to get the word out?"

I stumbled through what turned out to be not much of an answer. I don't know exactly why church planting is met with so much resistance from the very people, churches and leaders who clearly ought to be promoting it. But I do know this, we need to change that. We are out to change the church planting world.

THE KEY QUESTION:

Is there anything you are doing to sabotage
your church, judicatory or network?

THE BIG CHALLENGE:

Expect a bit of sabotage to occur in response
to the next big commitment you make.

CHAPTER THREE

WHY CHANGE THE WORLD?

*Very few people or companies can clearly articulate WHY
they do WHAT they do. When I say WHY, I don't mean to
make money - that's a result. By WHY I mean what is
your purpose, cause or belief? WHY does your company
exist? WHY do you get out of bed every morning? And
WHY should anyone care?*

—Simon Sinek, *Start with Why: How Great Leaders
Inspire Everyone to Take Action*

*Unless a man is ready to work for the salvation of others,
it may be questioned whether or not he himself is saved.
He who wants only enough religion to save himself is not
likely to have even that much.*

—Henry Turnbull

*The mission trumps. Always. Every time. In every conflict.
Not the pastor. Not the members of the church who pay
the bills. Not those who scream the loudest or who are
most in pain. No. In a healthy Christian ministry, the
mission wins every argument.*

—Tod Bolsinger

Charlie Brown is on the mound. He goes into his
windup and right before he throws the baseball,
his right fielder, Lucy, screams, "Charlie Brown,

ask the catcher if he loves me." Charlie is annoyed, but he asks the catcher, Schroeder, if he loves the right fielder, and Schroeder answers, "No, I don't." Charlie Brown gets back on the mound, he goes into his windup and right before he releases the ball, the right fielder screams, "Charlie Brown, ask the catcher why he doesn't love me." Charlie is pretty frustrated now, but he asks the catcher why he doesn't love the right fielder, to which Schroeder replies, "There are a hundred reasons why I don't love the right fielder." Again, Charlie Brown takes the mound. Again, he steps into his windup. But right before he pitches the ball the right fielder screams, "Charlie Brown, ask the catcher to name one reason why he doesn't love me." At his wits end, Charlie Brown storms out into right field and yells, "Can't we just play baseball?!" Lucy concludes, "Of course! That's why we're out here."

That story may not be all that funny, but it does raise a good question: Why? Why are we doing what we are doing? Why are we trying to change the church planting world?

Will Mancini wrote: "Ministry without clarity is insanity."

There's a verse from the Bible – an obscure verse, but one of my life verses that really sets the foundation for why we desperately need to change the church planting world. That verse is Acts 15:19:

> It is my judgment that we should not make it diffi-
> cult for the (people) who are turning to God.
>   —Acts 15:19

Jesus' brother James makes a statement that sums up the group's feelings. We should not make it difficult for people to turn to God. In this one sound bite, James makes at least four assumptions.

First Assumption

First, James assumes people are turning to God.

James simply believes that there are people who want to turn to God. More than that, he is referring to the Gentiles who are turning to God. Who were the Gentiles? Obviously, they were people who were not Jewish. But more than that, the **We should not make it difficult for people to turn to God.** term denoted pagans, heathens, uncircumcised, unclean dogs. To a Jewish person in the first century, to someone like James, the Gentiles were the last people they would have even expected to turn to God. But James admits people – even people we least expect – are turning to God.

Where did James get an assumption like that? Maybe from Jesus:

> Then he said to his disciples, "The harvest is plentiful but the workers are few."
> —Matthew 9:37 (NIV)

A scuba diver was enjoying the aquatic world twenty feet below the water line when he noticed another man the same depth—but he had no scuba gear at all. The diver went below another twenty feet, but moments later the same guy joined him. The diver went down another twenty-five feet, but again the other guy showed up! This confused the scuba diver, so he took out a waterproof chalkboard set and wrote, "How are you able to stay under the deep without any equipment?" The guy took the chalkboard and wrote, "I'm drowning!"

Many people realize they are in trouble and they want to turn to God. I wanted to turn to God. I'm guessing there was a moment you wanted to turn to God, as well.

When I was a student at UCLA, I joined a fraternity and got to see everything the world had to offer—the sex, and the drugs, and the rock and roll. I remember going to the frat parties, taking a step back and thinking, "There's got to be more to life than this."

I turned to God, and soon so did about a dozen fraternity brothers. Some people suggested that kind of spiritual revival experience would never happen again. But I've seen people turn to God ever since.

In our second church plant, we moved in as a "parachute drop." We didn't know anyone in town. The first person I met in the area described himself this way: "I am a thirty-two-year-old recovering alcoholic and co-dependent drug-addict, but I stopped drinking and doing drugs four months ago." When I asked why he stopped he admitted, "Somebody's been working in my life, and I think it might be Jesus." Then he said something that startled me: "And I'm sure there's a lot more people out there just like me."

"Somebody's been working in my life, and I think it might be Jesus. And I'm sure there's a lot more people out there just like me."

It keeps happening. A friend of mine, Anthony, showed up at our church a few months back. Anthony was having extreme marital problems. His wife let him know that their marriage was over. The one big thing they had in common was drug use, but after suffering through the consequences of that – financial difficulties, their teenage daughter moving out, the loss of jobs, Anthony was trying to get back on his feet. So he came to church, and he came to Christ, committing his life to following Jesus. Then his wife turned to God. People are turning to God.

> One of my main issues with some of the new models for church planting is they assume no one is interested.

In a recent edition of the *Sacramento Bee* there was an article highlighting how *Seventeen* magazine now has a section on faith. Laurie Whaley of Thomas Nelson Publishers said, "The teen culture today, they're very, very much about faith."

So, why do we expect them to not be interested in spiritual things?

One of my main issues with some of the new models for church planting is they assume no one is interested. Too many of us have slipped into thinking that everyone is resisting God, but that isn't true. Sure, some resist. But there are people out there who are quietly, if not desperately unsatisfied with their lives. They know there has to be more to life than this. They sense the emptiness. They are looking for God. But we miss them if we don't expect them.

From a passenger ship, everyone can see a bearded man on a small island who is shouting and desperately waving his hands. "Who is it?" a passenger asks the captain. "I've no idea," the captain admits. "But every year when we pass, he goes nuts."

Are we missing the people who are turning to God?

Second Assumption

Second, James assumes that believers can, and do, and maybe even have a tendency to make it difficult for people to turn to God.

James may have agreed with the quip, "Keep the faith… just not from others."

In Acts chapter 15 the barrier the believers put up had to do with rules and regulations:

> Some people came from Judea and started teaching the Lord's followers that they could not be saved, unless they were circumcised as Moses had taught. This caused trouble, *[ya think?]* and Paul and Barnabas argued with them about this teaching. So it was decided to send Paul and Barnabas and a few others to Jerusalem to discuss this problem with the apostles and the church leaders.
>
> —Acts 15:1-2 (CEV)

The believers were requiring circumcision for salvation. Ouch. Can you imagine the commotion that requirement would cause in the church's membership class? The book, *Why Men Hate Going to Church* would take on an entirely different meaning. The prerequisite of minor surgery on one's private parts would certainly slow down church growth. But James announced that this procedure wasn't necessary.

I don't know of a modern day North American Christian Church that requires circumcision for membership, but I do know that we in the church have a tendency to put up significant, if not similar, barriers.

Why People Say They Don't Go to Church
Do you know why people in the United States say they don't go to church? I've been compiling a decades-long informal survey and here is what I have found:

Number 5: The church is negative.
Ray Johnston wrote, "When you walk into the average church, it is so somber, so lifeless, it makes you want to ask, 'Who died?' not 'Who lived?'"[1]

> It reminds me of a story about a person at an old-fashioned church who actually died during a Sunday service. The paramedics were called. They ended up carrying out five people before finding the one who was actually dead.

Bradley R.E. Wright, in his book, *Christians Are Hate-Filled Hypocrites...and Other Lies You've Been Told: A Sociologist Shatters Myths From the Secular and Christian Media,* concluded, "Of all the groups, who has

---

1 Ray Johnston, *Jesus Called – He Wants His Church Back: What Christians and the American Church Are Missing,* Kindle Edition (Thomas Nelson, 2016).

the most negative attitude? Unfortunately, it seems to be Evangelicals."[2]

John Steinbeck captured this ailment for us as he described his character Liza Hamilton in *East of Eden*. "A tight, hard little woman, humorless as a chicken...She had a code of morals that pinned down and beat the brains out of nearly everything that was pleasant to do...She was suspicious of fun whether it involved dancing or singing or even laughter. She felt that people having a good time were wide open to the devil."[3]

Prolific Christian author, Leonard Sweet, tells his story: "When I was seventeen I de-converted from Christianity. Some people can give the date and time and place of their conversion. I can give the place (Sarasota Springs, New York), date (Pine Grove summer camp meeting), and time (Sunday morning's 'Big preaching' service during the altar-call hymn 'Softly and Tenderly') of my de-conversion... What ignited my de-conversion was the church's funeral spirit, its fussy-buttoned-up-ness. Christians' stay-at-home-and-pickle-in-their-own-juices personalities, their vinegary countenances drained me emotionally, incapacitated me intellectually, and shut me down spiritually. The best I could say was this: by and large, Christians were kind people in a bad mood."

Sheldon Vanauken summed it up with this classic quote: "The best argument for Christianity is Christians: their joy, their certainty, their completeness. But the

---

2   Bradley R.E. Wright, *Christians Are Hate-Filled Hypocrites. . . and Other Lies You've Been Told: A Sociologist Shatters Myths From the Secular and Christian Media* (Bethany House Publishers, 2010).

3   John Steinbeck, *East of Eden*, Reissue Edition (Penguin Classics, 1952).

strongest argument against Christianity is also Christians – when they are somber and joyless, when they are self-righteous and smug in complacent consecration, when they are narrow and repressive, then Christianity dies a thousand deaths."[4]

People don't want to feel bad, so when our services are known for making people feel bad, people stay away. Many people feel that the church is sad and gloomy and all they talk about is death.

Number 4: The sermons are long and boring.

It's been said, "There is a thin line between a long church service and a hostage situation."

Did you hear about the man who got up during the pastor's sermon, left, then came back right before it ended. "Where did you go during my sermon?" the pastor asked. "I went to get a haircut," the man admitted "Why didn't you get a haircut before the sermon?' the pastor demanded. The man concluded, "Before the sermon I didn't need a haircut."

An older gentleman went to his doctor for help with a snoring problem. "Does the snoring bother your wife?' the doctor asked. "Not really," the man admitted. "It's the rest of the congregation that finds it annoying."

In his book, *Talk Like TED*, Carmine Gallo has an entire chapter devoted to why TED Talks must be no longer than eighteen minutes. He reveals, "The longer the presentation, the more the listener has to organize, comprehend,

---

4   Sheldon Vanauken, *A Severe Mercy* (HarperOne, 2009).

and remember. The burden increases along with a listener's anxiety. They become increasingly frustrated, even angry."[5]

Albert Einstein once said, "If you can't explain it simply, you don't understand it well enough."

Number 3: All the church wants is my money.

An airplane was headed for a crash landing. Everyone was panicking, when the flight attendant turned to a passenger and screamed, "You're a pastor…do something religious!" So he took an offering.

Jesus talked a lot about money. He implied that we can tell a lot about a person by how they spend their income. But somehow the church has picked up this reputation for being money-hungry. I suspect that when churches and denominations are not generous toward funding new churches it only adds to the stereotype of the miserly church and it keeps the unchurched away.

Number 2: Everyone is a hypocrite.

The definition of a hypocrite isn't just someone who makes mistakes. That's the definition of a human being. The definition of a hypocrite is someone who makes mistakes, yet pretends to be perfect. That is more common than it ought to be in the North American church.

A little boy came running into the living room, "Mommy, Mommy," he gasped. "I found a mouse out in the garage, so I took the broom and smacked him in the head with it. Then I whacked him up against the wall, and

---

5   Carmine Gallo, *Talk Like TED: The 9 Public-Speaking Secrets of the World's Top Minds* (St. Martin's Griffin, 2015).

then I golfed him against the other wall…" Just then the boy realized that the pastor of his church was there talking to his mom. So the boy changed his tune and concluded, "And then the Lord called him home."

We in the church like to act like we are perfect, but we're not fooling anyone. We actually have to admit we need help for our problems to get into the "club," yet when we get to church, we pretend that we have no problems at all. It is ridiculous.

And when we do things like making it difficult for leaders to start churches, firing people who want to plant churches, and refusing to support church planters because we feel we're in competition with them, we show our hyper-hypocrisy.

Number 1: Church is irrelevant.

A father and son were riding in their truck together one day and the son asked the father, "Dad, how high can you count?" The father replied, "Well, I don't know, son – how high can you count?" The son immediately replied, "One thousand, five hundred, forty-two." The father pushed, "Why did you stop?" The son shrugged his shoulders and said, "Well, church was over."

Many see church as a waste of time, a ritual that doesn't make any difference. The music is out of date, the programs are out of tune and the sermons are out of touch with the real world.

We don't mean to produce irrelevant services, but many of us were simply trained that way. Fred Craddock in his book, *Preaching,* admits about preachers, "Their seminary experience of theology was not one of learning to think theologically but one of spending two terms in the fourth century."[6]

The newly appointed pastor announced to the old, traditional congregation in his first sermon, "It is my goal to bring this church into the twentieth century!" Someone from the back row yelled, "Don't you mean twenty-first century?" The pastor replied, "We'll take it one century at a time."

When we pause to look at those top reasons why people don't go to church: irrelevancy, hypocrisy, money, boredom, and negativity, we see that people are not necessarily rejecting God as much as the packaging that we have put him in. People are not saying that they don't want to turn to God, instead they are saying that church people might be making it difficult for them to turn to God.

Third Assumption

James makes a *third* assumption in Acts 15, verse 18: *It is not difficult to turn to God.*

Peter says,

> So turn to God! Give up your sins, and you will be forgiven.
>
> —Acts 3:19 (CEV)

Jesus promised,

---

6   Fred B. Craddock, *Preaching* (Abingdon Press, 2010).

Come to me, all of you who are weary and carry heavy burdens, and I will give you rest. Take my yoke upon you. Let me teach you, because I am humble and gentle at heart, and you will find rest for your souls. For my yoke is easy to bear, and the burden I give you is light.

—Matthew 11:28-29 (NLT)

It is not difficult to turn to God.

Tom Mercer, in his classic work, *8 to 15: The World is Smaller than You Think*, says turning to Jesus is as simple as the ABCs:

A. *Admit* I have fallen short and need a Savior. I need to turn to God

B. *Believe* that Jesus is the Savior   He came to earth, lived a perfect life as our example; went to the cross and died to pay the penalty for my sins; and rose again from the dead to prove it. God is there, waiting for me to turn to Him.

C. *Commit* to following Him the best I can for the rest of my life. Choose to turn to God.[7]

---

7   Tom Mercer, *8 to 15: The World is Smaller than You Think* (Oikos Books, 2011).

My son Tim observes that many of us pray the "ABR Prayer." We *admit* we need help, we even *believe* Jesus offers it, but then we simply *resume* living the way we were living.

Turning to God isn't difficult. It's not easy street, but we don't have to be mystified and stymied by it.

If you are turning to God, but have never made that choice to commit your life to Jesus, I would encourage you to admit your need to God, believe Jesus offers you forgiveness, and commit right now to following Jesus the best you can for the rest of your life.

When Houdini, that great escape artist was in his heyday, he issued a nationwide challenge. The Great Houdini claimed he could break out of any locked quarters in one hour or less – on one condition: no one was allowed to watch him work. One prison took Houdini up on his offer. They escorted Houdini amidst remarkable fanfare to their institution. They led him to an isolated cell, placed him in it, turned the key and proceeded to another section of the prison to await the great escape. As soon as the officials left, Houdini took out all the tools he'd smuggled in (that's why he didn't want anyone watching) and started in. But the tools weren't effective. Fifteen minutes into the ordeal he was still in the cell. Thirty minutes went by. Forty minutes passed. An hour ticked by on the clock. After an hour and ten minutes, in absolute frustration, Houdini leaned up against the cell door. And guess what happened? The door opened right up. It hadn't even been locked. The Great Houdini was stopped because he assumed the task was far greater than it actually was.

The same is true for many of us. We've not turned to God because we believe it is way more complicated than it truly is.

Fourth Assumption

There is a *fourth* assumption James makes in Acts 15:19: James assumes *we can make a difference.*

James assumes that what the early church people did, and what we do, actually makes a big difference in the lives of others.

P.T. Barnum revealed, "Without promotion, something terrible happens…nothing!"

Teenager Matthew Boya decided to practice his golf swing on a field next to an air base in the country of Benin, Africa. He took one swing and sliced his shot way off to his right. The golf ball struck a low-flying sea gull and knocked it unconscious. As the sea gull started to fall toward the ground it slammed into the windshield of a trainer jet that was taxiing into position for takeoff. The impact of the bird caused the pilot to lose control of his aircraft, which then plowed into four shiny Mirage jets that were parked along the runway. The trainer jet and the Mirage jets were all greatly damaged or destroyed. Unfortunately, the entire air force of Benin, Africa consisted of that trainer and those four Mirage jets.[8]

Matthew Boya did over $40 million worth of damage, and that was in 1987 dollars. Think of the impact you and I can make.

---

8   Michael L. Williams, *Stranger Than Fiction: The Lincoln Curse, Volume 1* (CreateSpace Independent Publishing Platform, 2012).

C. Peter Wagner stated, "The single most effective evangelistic methodology under heaven is planting new churches."

> Donald McGavran said the best way to evangelize a caste is not for a foreigner to preach to them. He concluded the best way to reach "untouchables" was to plant a church in their culture and have members of that church who were "untouchable" to evangelize their friends, neighbors, relatives, and associates. Church planting resulted in "untouchables" evangelizing "untouchables."[9]
>
> —Elmer Towns

Just think how much of a difference we could make. If we change the church planting world, we will change many people's worlds.

Let's heed the words of Jesus:

> Then he said to his disciples, "The harvest is plentiful but the workers are few. Ask the Lord of the harvest, therefore, to send out workers into his harvest field."
>
> —Matthew 9:37-38 (NIV)

We can ask and we can be part of sending out workers into God's harvest field.

---

9   Elmer L. Towns, *Putting an End to Worship Wars* (Broadman & Holman Publishers, 1997).

The *why* of church planting is obvious – we need more churches because people are turning to God!

THE KEY QUESTION:

Is an expectation that people really are turning to God actually a part of my ministry vision?

THE BIG CHALLENGE:

Come up with at least one reason in addition to JD's top five for why people may not be attending church.

CHAPTER FOUR

NO TEA FOR ME

No matter what people tell you, words and ideas can change the world.

—Robin Williams

Every great dream begins with a dreamer. Always remember, you have within you the strength, the patience, and the passion to reach for the stars to change the world.

—Harriet Tubman

Great companies start because the founders want to change the world...not make a fast buck.

—Guy Kawasaki

An Anglican cleric is credited with quipping, "Everywhere the Apostle Paul went there was a revival or a riot. Everywhere I go they serve tea."

We want to stop sipping tea and start turning the church planting world on its ear. We want to change the church planting world. But how could we possibly do that?

In the book of the Acts of the Apostles we see a better picture of the church Jesus founded, established and envisioned. And there is one watershed verse that sums up the entire book:

> These who have turned the world upside down have
> come here too.
>
> —Acts 17:6 (NKJV)

The apostles turned their world upside down. Their world was broken, and they turned it upside down. Their church was non-existent, yet in seventeen chapters they turned it around.

How Did They Change Their World?

How did they do it? What did they do? What can we do?

Let's start looking through the book of Acts for some clues on how the early church leaders turned their world upside down in only a few chapters.

1. They were consistently filled with the Holy Spirit

There was one characteristic of the early church leaders that appears first and seems to set the pace for everything else that occurred. There was one trait of the early church leaders and people that caused them to turn everything around. And we see it at the beginning of the book of Acts:

> During the forty days after he suffered and died, he
> appeared to the apostles from time to time, and he
> proved to them in many ways that he was actually
> alive. And he talked to them about the Kingdom
> of God. Once when he was eating with them,
> he commanded them, "Do not leave Jerusalem
> until the Father sends you the gift he promised, as

I told you before. John baptized with water, but in just a few days you will be baptized with the Holy Spirit."

—Acts 1:3-5 (NLT)

But you will receive power when the Holy Spirit comes upon you. And you will be my witnesses, telling people about me everywhere—in Jerusalem, throughout Judea, in Samaria, and to the ends of the earth.

—Acts 1:8 (NLT)

Jesus promised to send the Holy Spirit to his followers. Then the promise was fulfilled:

And everyone present was filled with the Holy Spirit...

—Acts 2:4 (NLT)

Peter continued:

What you see was predicted long ago by the prophet Joel: "'In the last days,' God says, 'I will pour out my Spirit upon all people. Your sons and daughters will prophesy. Your young men will see visions, and your old men will dream dreams. In those days I will pour out my Spirit even on my servants—men and women alike—and they will prophesy.'"

—Acts 2:16-18 (NLT)

The early leaders turned the world upside down because they were consistently filled with the Holy Spirit.

The Holy Spirit is mentioned forty-seven times in the book of Acts. The believers didn't really turn things around, the Holy Spirit turned things around. Maybe instead of "Acts of the Apostles," the book could be called, "Acts of the Holy Spirit through the Apostles."

The Holy Spirit is a mysterious topic.

Now I realize that the Holy Spirit is a mysterious topic.

We don't talk all that much about the Holy Spirit. The Holy Spirit is like the kid brother of the Trinity. You have the Father, and the Son, and then the little rascal that doesn't get much attention.

In my Irish heritage the leaders seemed to say, "In the name of the Father, and of the Son, and whoever comes after that..."

We don't need to fret because we don't understand the Holy Spirit. After all, we don't even understand the opposite sex, we don't understand what a catch is now in the NFL, we don't understand the electoral college or how to graduate from it!

The Holy Spirit is also a scary topic.

Many people respond to the Holy Spirit with fear, maybe because for centuries the English translation was, "Holy Ghost." We're living in an era of, "Who you gonna call? Ghostbusters!" So this powerful being in our lives can be scary.

I had a linebacker coach in high school who had a reputation for being a very scary dude. Players stayed away from him. But when we linebackers went off for our position drills, that coach became amazingly friendly. He treated us like sons, like family, and like all-stars. There was nothing he wouldn't do for us. Our God is an awesome God, yet when we realize his love for us, when we realize he treats us like family, like sons and daughters, princes and princesses, we feel his perfect love cast out fear.

The Holy Spirit is a controversial topic.

Few subjects have evoked the heated debates within Christianity like the Holy Spirit has. Some groups feel that you can't be a real Christian unless you have some second blessing from the Holy Spirit that results in speaking in tongues. Other denominations say that the work of the Holy Spirit has basically stopped.

The early church leaders did not argue about what it meant to be filled with the Holy Spirit... They were simply filled.

The early church leaders did not argue about what it meant to be filled with the Holy Spirit. They didn't engage in theological arguments about how one manifestation of filling was better than another. They didn't insist that some specific indicators of the Spirit's power were no longer in existence. They were simply filled.

Mark Driscoll told me the controversy can subside when we realize that the Book of Acts isn't a stand-alone work – it is part of a larger effort.

The Book of Acts begins this way:

> In my former book, Theophilus, I wrote about all
> that Jesus began to do and to teach until the day
> he was taken up to heaven, after giving instruc-
> tions through the Holy Spirit to the apostles he had
> chosen.
>
> —Acts 1:1-2 (NIV)

The Book of Acts is actually a sequel. Luke is dedicat-
ing these books to his trusted friend, Theophilus. His first
book started out like this:

> Many have undertaken to draw up an account
> of the things that have been fulfilled among us,
> just as they were handed down to us by those who
> from the first were eyewitnesses and servants of
> the word. With this in mind, since I myself have
> carefully investigated everything from the begin-
> ning, I too decided to write an orderly account for
> you, most excellent Theophilus, so that you may
> know the certainty of the things you have been
> taught.
>
> —Luke 1:1-4 (NIV)

Early on, Luke wrote:

> One day when the crowds were being baptized,
> Jesus himself was baptized. As he was praying, the
> heavens opened, and the Holy Spirit, in bodily
> form, descended on him like a dove.
>
> —Luke 3:21-22 (NLT)

So Acts is a continuation of the book of Luke. Acts is the sequel. In Luke, we read about all the things Jesus did with the power of the Holy Spirit in him. In Acts, Luke sets it up so we can read about all the things the apostles also did through the power of the Holy Spirit.

God poured out his Holy Spirit, and they received him and were filled. They didn't mandate to God how and when and by what process or order he had to give them his gift. They simply opened their lives to the Holy Spirit, and they listened and then followed – consistently.

2. They were relentlessly committed to leadership development

Let's get back to Acts chapter 1. Peter continued:

> "So now we must choose a replacement for Judas from among the men who were with us the entire time we were travelling with the Lord Jesus – from the time he was baptized by John until the day he was taken from us. Whoever is chosen will join us as a witness of Jesus' resurrection." So they nominated two men: Joseph called Barsabbas (also known as Justus) and Matthias. Then they all prayed, "O Lord, you know every heart. Show us which of these men you have chosen as an apostle to replace Judas in this ministry, for he has deserted us and gone where he belongs." Then they cast lots, and Matthias was selected to become an apostle with the other eleven.
>
> —Acts 1:20-26 (NLT)

The early church leaders were dedicated to leadership development. I suspect that most of us would have been fine with eleven leaders. We realize it is necessary to downsize sometimes. Okay, there is something special, from a Biblical view, about the number twelve; there were twelve tribes, and the number was used 176 times in the Bible. But aren't eleven solid leaders just as good as twelve?

Throughout the book of Acts, we see the leaders enlarging their entourage of leaders.

Apparently not. They needed another leader.

Nothing stopped them from developing leaders, not even major differences:

> Their disagreement was so sharp that they separated. Barnabas took John Mark with him and sailed for Cyprus. Paul chose Silas, and as he left, the believers entrusted him to the Lord's gracious care.
>
> —Acts 15:39-40 (NLT)

Their mantra was, "No soup for you! Next!" We're trying to get back to looking for leaders.

Throughout the book of Acts, we see the leaders enlarging their entourage of leaders:

> Several men were traveling with him. They were Sopater son of Pyrrhus from Berea; Aristarchus and Secundus from Thessalonica; Gaius from Derbe; Timothy; and Tychicus and Trophimus from the province of Asia.
>
> —Acts 20:4 (NLT)

Bob Briner says, "Almost from the first day he was with them, Jesus told his followers that he would be with them only a short time. From time to time they argued with Him about the limited tenure he described, but He continued to reiterate that His time with them would be very limited…Both through His actions and His teachings, Jesus demonstrated that He expected His followers to be fruitful and productive. He was un-equivocating on this."

Kevin Myers added, "If you're committed to Scripture, you will build a leadership culture."

3. They persistently adopted simple structures

> Then they cast lots, and Matthias was selected to become an apostle with the other eleven.
>
> —Acts 1:20-26 (NLT)

Flipping a coin works better than a search committee.

Albert Camus once said, "Integrity has no need of rules."

Larry Osborne suggested, "Policy is a de-motivator, have as few as possible." Osborne also quipped that the structural methodology of the early church consisted of making things up as they went along!

Peter Drucker concluded: "I just know that the more control there is, the less growth there is."

> Select seven men who are well respected and are full of the Spirit and wisdom… Everyone liked this idea…
>
> —Acts 6:3 & 5 (NLT)

It was a simple idea. And look at the result:

> So God's message continued to spread. The number
> of believers greatly increased in Jerusalem…
> —Acts 6:7 (NLT)

The leaders' simple structure set up sustained growth.

I suspect your structure is too complicated. Our church staff worked through the book, *Simple Church*, and found that book to be way too cumbersome.

I'm serving on the board of one of our church plants – we're in a dual affiliation situation – and one of the first items for the board was: "To adopt a statement of Executive Limitations to establish limitations on the authority of the Lead Pastor."

I may have missed it, but I don't think they adopted a "statement of Executive Limitations" for Matthias. In Acts 13, I must have overlooked the verses where the Antioch church established limitations on the authority of Paul and Barnabas.

> **I must have overlooked the verses where the Antioch church established limitations on the authority of Paul and Barnabas.**

A golfer walks into the pro shop at the local course and asks the golf pro if they sell ball markers. The golf pro says they do, and they cost one dollar. The guy gives the golf pro a dollar. The golf pro opens the register, puts in the dollar, then hands him a quarter.

The early church leaders simply simplified.

4. They were constantly together

> When the day of Pentecost came, they were all together in one place.
>
> —Acts 2:1 (NIV)

> And all the believers met together in one place and shared everything they had.
>
> —Acts 2:44 (NLT)

The early church leaders were together. Paul and Barnabas were sent out from the Antioch Church in Acts chapter 13, but at the end of chapter 14, they returned to the Antioch church for updates, reports and encouragement.

Even when Paul was traveling, he took time to hang out with other believers and leaders.

> We went ashore, found the local believers, and stayed with them a week.
>
> —Acts 21:4 (NLT)

> The next day when we docked at Sidon, Julius was very kind to Paul and let him go ashore to visit with friends so they could provide for his needs.
>
> —Acts 27:3 (NLT)

I suspect the apostles got the idea of being together from their time with Jesus.

The time Jesus invested in these few disciples was so much more by comparison to that given to others that it can only be regarded as a deliberate strategy. He actually spent more time with his disciples than with everyone else in the world combined.[10]

—Robert Coleman

5. They were joyfully resilient

But others in the crowd ridiculed them, saying, "They're just drunk, that's all!"

—Acts 2:13 (NLT)

If we are fortunate, we can make it for a chapter and thirteen verses before we start getting ridiculed.

They arrested them and, since it was already evening, put them in jail until morning.

—Acts 4:3 (NLT)

We should expect to be arrested about every four chapters. And Stephen's stoning by his enemies suggests someone might get killed about every seven chapters.

The apostles left the Sanhedrin, rejoicing because they had been counted worthy of suffering disgrace for the Name.

—Acts 5:41 (NIV)

---

10   Robert Coleman, *The Master Plan of Evangelism* (Revell, 2010).

In Acts 5, the leaders rejoiced because they were worthy of suffering.

In Acts 13, Paul and Barnabas get sent off, and they came to another Antioch. Almost the whole town comes out to hear them, many come to Christ, and the chapter ends with them getting run out of town – and they were filled with joy and the Holy Spirit. They loved it, or at least they expected trouble.

Church Planter Rusty Price said, "When they are shooting at you, sometimes you just need to keep your head down and your butt up!"

> Men will never become great in divinity until they become great in suffering. "Ah!" said Luther, "affliction is the best book in my library;" and let me add, the best leaf in the book of affliction is that blackest of all the leaves, the leaf called heaviness, when the spirit sinks within us, and we cannot endure as we could wish. And yet again; this heaviness is of essential use to a Christian, if he would do good to others.... There are none so tender as those who have been skinned themselves. Those who have been in the chamber of affliction know how to comfort those who are there.
>
> —Charles Spurgeon

6. They were extremely generous

> They sold their property and possessions and shared the money with those in need.
>
> —Acts 2:45 (NLT)

> All the believers were united in heart and mind. And
> they felt that what they owned was not their own,
> so they shared everything they had… There were
> no needy people among them, because those who
> owned land or houses would sell them and bring the
> money to the apostles to give to those in need.
>
> —Acts 4:32-35 (NLT)

> So the believers in Antioch decided to send relief to
> the brothers and sisters in Judea, everyone giving as
> much as they could. This they did, entrusting their
> gifts to Barnabas and Saul to take to the elders of
> the church in Jerusalem.
>
> —Acts 11:29-30 (NLT)

All throughout the book of Acts we see the disciples practicing significant generosity.

My son Scott, owner of Seek First Financial, is an economic guru, he says, "Seeking the kingdom first starts with giving. Give wholeheartedly and trust God for the outcome. You'll be amazed at what happens."

Chapter 5 of Acts is a story of sin, of dishonesty, and conspiracy, but it also gives us a pretty good idea of what God thinks of selfishness, greediness, and a lack of generosity.

7. They were likeably bold

> So they called the apostles back in and commanded
> them never again to speak or teach in the name of
> Jesus. But Peter and John replied, "Do you think God

wants us to obey you rather than him? We cannot
stop telling about everything we have seen and heard."
—Acts 4:18-19 (NLT)

After this prayer, the meeting place shook, and
they were all filled with the Holy Spirit. Then they
preached the word of God with boldness.
—Acts 4:31 (NLT)

The book of Acts ends with Paul's boldness:

He bravely preached about God's kingdom and
taught about the Lord Jesus Christ, and no one
tried to stop him.
—Acts 28:31 (CEV)

In the past couple of weeks I have had two different
struggling, reticent church planters at different times in
different cities tell me this exact phrase: "I don't want to
pick a fight with the devil."

It is too late for that! The fight is on! We have two
choices; be miserable because we've chosen to try to be
comfortable, or be joyful in the midst of the fight because
we know we're on the winning side.

We have to be bold, and we can actually be bold and
likeable at the same time.

Likeability
"I'd rather be respected than liked." Whenever I hear that
statement I wonder why those are the only two options

mentioned. Sometimes a parent says, "My job is to be his father, not his friend." I think, "Seriously, are those two mutually exclusive?" And when I hear a boss declare, "I want my employees to fear me, not like me," I think we must be missing something.

A verse from the Book of Acts may surprise us here:

> The apostles worked many miracles and wonders among the people. All of the Lord's followers often met in the part of the temple known as Solomon's Porch. No one outside their group dared join them, even though *everyone liked them very much.*
>
> —Acts 5:12-13 (CEV)

Did you catch that? Everyone liked the early Christians very much. Okay, so not everyone joined them. Some even tried to destroy them – but they were likeable.

Don Marquis observed, "Some persons are likeable in spite of their unswerving integrity."

If we're going to excel as leaders we cannot be people pleasers, but we must be likeable. If we're not likeable, sooner or later, someone who doesn't like us will gather enough folks who don't like us and we will not like the result—we'll be out of business.

Check out the very next verse in Acts 5:

> Many men and women started having faith in the Lord.
>
> —Acts 5:14 (CEV)

The early church leaders were likeable and bold, and many people turned to God.

Dale Carnegie, in his classic book, *How To Win Friends and Influence People*, reveals that getting along with your co-workers will not only improve our overall work experience, it will make us more successful.[11]

A study by Melinda Tamkins of Columbia University indicated that workplace effectiveness comes not so much by what or who you know but by your popularity. The study revealed: "Popular workers were seen as trustworthy, motivated, serious, decisive, and hardworking, and were recommended for fast-track promotion and generous pay increases. Their less-liked colleagues were perceived as arrogant, conniving and manipulative. Pay raises and promotions were ruled out regardless of their academic background or professional qualifications."

For years I've thought that our presidential elections have been won by the most likeable candidates among the top nominees—at least since 1968 when Richard Nixon beat the affable Hubert Humphrey.

The Gallup Company went a step further. They've conducted a personality poll prior to every recent presidential election and found that likeability has been the most consistent predictor of who would win since 1960!

Leadership must be likeable. If I want to be effective at leading people, I need to be effective with people.

---

11   Dale Carnegie, *How To Win Friends and Influence People* (General Press, 2016)

The Top Ten Signs Nobody Likes You[12]

10. You remind your teacher that she forgot to give homework.

9. Your dog refuses to be seen outside with you.

8. Your B.S. is in B.S.

7. Your imaginary friends keep finding excuses not to come over.

6. You are so annoying that even your multiple personalities won't speak to you anymore.

5. You've actually had Mormon missionaries tell you, "We've gotta get going now"

4. You're wearing a yellow shirt with a black zig zag about halfway down

3. You find yourself seated in a handbasket and getting warmer.

2. You often find yourself asking, "What would Vladimir Putin do?"

1. Randy Newman is singing "You've Got a Friend in Me" when he notices you in the crowd. Then he stops.

---

12 Adopted from "Christian's & Scott's Interactive Top Ten Lists"

Likeability is necessary for leadership. But likeability isn't necessarily a gift.

Travis Bradbury wrote: "In a study conducted at UCLA, subjects rated over 500 adjectives based on their perceived significance to likeability. The top-rated adjectives had nothing to do with being gregarious, intelligent, or attractive (innate characteristics). Instead, the top adjectives were sincerity, transparency, and capacity for understanding."

Likeability is a skill set. It can be learned; it can be developed.

So how do we get it?

Here is one suggestion as a place to start:

> But the fruit of the Spirit is love, joy, peace, forbearance, kindness, goodness, faithfulness, gentleness and self-control. Against such things there is no law.
>
> —Galatians 5:22-23 (NIV)

Let's start where the early followers of Christ started – let's ask God to forgive us and fill us with His Spirit. The result might just be an increase in our likeability.

The early church leaders turned the world upside down. They were filled with the Holy Spirit, committed to new leaders, set on keeping it simple, regularly meeting together, amazingly resilient, incredibly generous, and very bold.

But there was one other characteristic of the early church that helped them change things. We will look at that characteristic next.

THE KEY QUESTION:

How many of these seven characteristics of great leaders are consistent in your life? Your church? Your network?

THE BIG CHALLENGE:

Ask someone you trust to rate you on the seven characteristics in this section. Ask them for feedback on how you can improve in whatever areas necessary.

CHAPTER FIVE

THE OTHER WAY

The Pessimist complains about the wind.
The Optimist expects it to change.
The Leader adjusts the sails.

We all want progress, but if you're on the wrong road,
progress means doing an about-turn and walking back
to the right road; in that case, the man who turns back
soonest is the most progressive.

—C.S. Lewis

Success is simple. Do what's right, the right way, at the
right time.

—Arnold H. Glasow

D uring college as I was working at Ralphs grocery store in Century City, California. Whenever something would go obviously wrong, one of our store managers would walk over, put his hands on his hips, and state sarcastically, "Do it the other way." New employees would always ask, "What's the other way?" The manager would respond with a smirk, "The right way."

The early church leaders did ministry the other way – the right way.

LEADING THE OTHER WAY

These who have turned the world upside down have come here too.

—Acts 17:6 (NKJV)

What was their way?

One critical characteristic of the church leaders for turning the world upside down is *they had a clear strategy.* That strategy, and our philosophy of church planting comes from Acts 13, which describes the beginning of church planting in the Bible, and it also describes their pattern for planting.

> In the church at Antioch there were prophets and teachers: Barnabas, Simeon called Niger, Lucius of Cyrene, Manaen (who had been brought up with Herod the tetrarch) and Saul. While they were worshiping the Lord and fasting, the Holy Spirit said, 'Set apart for me Barnabas and Saul for the work to which I have called them.' So after they had fasted and prayed, they placed their hands on them and sent them off.
>
> —Acts 13:1-3

These first few verses of Acts 13 point to a four-fold strategy for church planting:

1. Spot high-level leaders.

There are high-level leaders out there. Just as there were high-level leaders in the early church, there are high-level leaders in existence today. We are finding trailblazers created, called, and equipped by God for significant ministries.

Of course we know that Jesus said, "The harvest is plentiful, but the workers are few" (Matthew 9:37).

But Jesus didn't say that the workers are extinct. He didn't say they don't exist. He said they are few – but they are out there and we are trying to spot them. We are looking for the Barnabases (Barnabi?) and Sauls of the present day.

> **Just as there were high-level leaders in the early church, there are high-level leaders in existence today.**

You might think, "We don't have Barnabases and Sauls in our church." Maybe you actually do. Back in Acts 11 we see:

> During this time some prophets came down from Jerusalem to Antioch. One of them, named Agabus, stood up and through the Spirit predicted that a severe famine would spread over the entire Roman world. (This happened during the reign of Claudius.) The disciples, as each one was able, decided to provide help for the brothers and sisters living in Judea. This they did, sending their gifts to the elders by Barnabas and Saul.
>
> —Acts 11:27-30 (NIV)

> When Barnabas and Saul had finished their mission, they returned from Jerusalem, taking with them John, also called Mark.
>
> —Acts 12:25 (NIV)

Barnabas and Saul started out by running an errand. They proved themselves as leaders and teachers, and so when the Holy Spirit said, "Set them apart…" the church could say, "Amen" rather than "Not so fast…"

Look for clues as to who are the church planters in your midst.

2. Set up high-level leaders for success.

Actually, the beginning of church planting may be better identified by what happened in Acts chapter 11:

> Now those who had been scattered by the persecution that broke out when Stephen was killed traveled as far as Phoenicia, Cyprus and Antioch, spreading the word only among Jews. Some of them, however, men from Cyprus and Cyrene, went to Antioch and began to speak to Greeks also, telling them the good news about the Lord Jesus. The Lord's hand was with them, and a great number of people believed and turned to the Lord. News of this reached the church in Jerusalem.
>
> —Acts 11:19-22a (NIV)

The persecution after the stoning of Stephen sparked new churches all over the first-century world. One of the most notable of these new churches was in Antioch, and the notoriety came from its rapid growth. But it was also known for another reason: A lot of Greeks and non-Jews, (Gentiles) were involved.

The Jerusalem church found out about the new church doing things in a different city, in a different way, and targeting a different crowd. The way the church in Jerusalem responded to this is one of the most brilliant, strategic, world-changing actions ever made:

> News of this reached the church in Jerusalem, and
> they sent Barnabas to Antioch.
> —Acts 11:22 (NIV)

The Jerusalem church sent Barnabas. They sent Mr. Encouragement. They sent someone to fan the flames, not douse them.

The Jerusalem church could have very easily sent a third-string, bean-counting, denominational representative. They could have sent the message, "I'm sorry, we don't do church that way. We don't have those kinds of people in our congregation. No Jews? No church for you!" The home office didn't try to control things, and they didn't try to contain things. They sent the most encouraging person they had – Barnabas.

Leadership isn't about tenure, titles, or even authority. If we are good, full of the Holy Spirit and full of faith, great things will happen.

> They sent Barnabas to Antioch. When he arrived and saw what the grace of God had done, he was glad and encouraged them all to remain true to the Lord with all their hearts. He was a good man, full

of the Holy Spirit and faith, and a great number of
people were brought to the Lord.

—Acts 11:23-24 (NIV)

Barnabas showed up with gladness and encouragement.
He not only said, "You've got a great thing going here," he
also stepped in and helped out.

In this passage we see clear job qualifications for those
who work in leadership settings: he was a good man, full
of the Holy Spirit and full of faith. Leadership isn't about
tenure, titles, or even authority. If we are good, full of the
Holy Spirit and full of faith, great things will happen.

Barnabas didn't stop with encouragement and helping.
He had an idea:

Then Barnabas went to Tarsus to look for Saul, and
when he found him, he brought him to Antioch.
So for a whole year Barnabas and Saul met with the
church and taught great numbers of people. The
disciples were called Christians first at Antioch.

—Acts 11:25-28 (NIV)

Barnabas spotted a high-level leader in Saul, and set
him up for success. The encourager created a safe place for
Saul to grow into an effective leader. Paul Borden says this
of unseasoned pastors, "Everyone needs a place to be bad."
Borden suggests a good place to be bad is on the staff of a
growing fruitful church.[13]

---

13   Paul D. Borden, *Make or Break Your Church in 365 Days: A Daily Guide to Leading Effective Change*
(Abingdon Press, 2012).

The disciples were first called "Christians" in Antioch. I sense that is more than just a simple descriptive statement. The Antioch church put Christianity on the map. In Antioch, Christianity went from a small, segregated sect to an inter-cultural movement. In Antioch, Christianity went from a Jerusalem group to an inter-continental effort. In Antioch, Christianity went from an unknown clique to an international phenomenon.

> **In Antioch, Christianity went from an unknown clique to an international phenomenon.**

3. Send out high-level leaders.

We also see that in Acts chapter 13.

> So after they had fasted and prayed, they placed their hands on them and sent them off.
>
> —Acts 13:1-3 (NIV)

What does it mean to lay or place hands on someone?

There's an *endorsing* element.

> We're not to lay hands on someone too hastily.
>
> —1 Timothy 5:22

> Then the apostles prayed and placed their hands on the men to show that they had been chosen to do this work.
>
> —Acts 6:6 (CEV)

When they laid hands on Barnabas and Saul, they were endorsing them. When we send out a church planter, we are letting them and everyone else know that we are for them, we are behind them, we are endorsing them.

We want to get to know candidates so we can actually, honestly affirm them and say, "We believe in these people."

That's why we require all planters that we work with to go through a "Discovery Center" to discover their best next steps. We want to get to know candidates so we can actually, honestly affirm them and say, "We believe in these people." They have our endorsement, our recommendation, our team stamp.

There's an *empowering* element.

When the disciples laid hands on someone, they received and/or were filled and empowered by the Holy Spirit. It appears they may have even received spiritual gifts through this. (1 Timothy 4, Acts 19)

When we send out a church planter we are saying that they have our resources, our backing, and our prayers. They are a part of us.

There's a *relational* element.

Acts 13 says that church planting is a team sport. Sure, there are a few individuals who will go it alone and plant a church without any backing or network. But we have to change that aspect of the church planting world.

4. Support high-level leaders.

When the Antioch church sent out Barnabas there was clear support; but one observation I've consistently seen in thirty-plus years in church is how little support there is for church planters. There's a lot of promises, a lot of buildup, and a lot of talk, but embarrassingly little support.

A few years ago I was asked to participate in a leadership group with other top church planting agencies in the United States. In our meetings, I noticed that actually supporting leaders appeared to be a missing ingredient in even the top agencies.

In the Excel Leadership Network we have worked hard to establish ten support systems or environments.

First is the *Spiritual Vitality* system.

The Psalmist wrote, "Unless the Lord builds the house, its builders labor in vain" (Psalm 127:1).

We can extrapolate that to: "Unless God builds the church, we're wasting everyone's time."

Jesus said, "Apart from me you can do nothing" (John 15:5).

Second is the *Funding* system.

Jesus warned,

> Suppose one of you wants to build a tower. Will he not first sit down and estimate the cost to see if he has enough money to complete it?
>
> —Luke 14:28

Ministry involves raising ministers, momentum, and money.

Our funding system utilizes these principles:

A. *We do investments, not grants.* We'll put money into a project, but we expect the money to come back to the network. It isn't a loan – it's an investment, because we're building a partnership, a movement.

B. *We invest based on matching funds.* We'll match what a planter raises (to a level agreed upon with the planter). The matching funds principle reinforces that if someone cannot raise money, they probably cannot plant a church. Also, the matching funds principle helps greatly in raising money.

C. *We do "incentive-laden" contracts.* Money is dispersed to the planter as certain agreed-upon milestones are met.

Third is the *Inviting* environment.

We work hard at attracting high-level church planters, leaders, and prospects to our movement.

Fourth is a *Discovery* environment.

In Ephesians chapter 4, the Apostle Paul talks about the body of Christ being built up for effective ministry.

He cites gifting, *"speaking the truth in love,"* and *"each part doing its work."* We need to make sure that a candidate is suited for the entrepreneurial leadership task of planting before we send them out.

I have seen too many church planters who were godly, gifted, and even well funded never get their projects off the ground. Why did they fail?

We offer one of the best (okay, I believe it is *the* best) church planting discovery structures in America – the Excel Leadership Network Discovery Center – a multi-day event to help potential planters see if this is the right ministry fit for them.

The fifth structure is the *Vision Alignment* system.

Solomon said, "It is not good to have zeal without knowledge or to be hasty and miss the way" (Proverbs 19:2 NIV).

I have seen too many church planters who were godly, gifted, and even well funded never get their projects off the ground. Why did they fail? They struggled because they were often sent out to the wrong place, or at the wrong time, or with the wrong team (usually with no team). Or they were sent out with strategies and tactics that might have been exciting and new, but stood no chance of succeeding.

We've put together a team of wise strategists who will interact with planters on their plans and proposals. We want to be fostering faith, yet eliminating as much needless risk as possible.

Sixth, we offer a *Training* environment.

Regretfully, most of the church planting training available today is underwhelming. The majority of planters survive by trial and error. We have put together our own training pieces, consisting of seminars, utilizing existing conferences and resources, but our primary training method is to send our trainers on site to work with the planter and the church plant team.

The seventh structure is a *Coaching* environment.

> For waging war you need guidance and for victory
> many advisers.
>> —Proverbs 24:6

We attempt to provide on-going, easily-accessible advice, counsel, and encouragement for the church planters we deploy. So, we've assembled a team of leaders experienced in church planting to walk with every church planter. The church planter gets to pick a coach from a number of highly successful planters and coaches.

In addition we offer an eighth structure: a *Caring* environment.

Most church planters feel at least somewhat abandoned. That is because they usually are abandoned. Typically, church planters are recruited, wined, dined, and then dropped behind enemy lines. If things don't go well, the sending agency begins by beating up the church planter. If it goes worse, all knowledge and involvement in the project is categorically denied by anyone who did any of the sending. If things do go well, the planter is often pushed aside while the glory is scooped up by the agency, which claims, "This was really all our idea all along!"

These feelings of being neglected and discarded can actually seem deeper for the church planter's spouse and family.

Church planters are on the front lines, the cutting edge of ministry. We try to care for them and treat them with honor (1 Timothy 5:17).

> It was there that they had been placed in God's care
> for the work…
>
> —Acts 14:26 (CEV)

Our primary caring structure consists of Connection Events, where we bring planters together for prayer, training, and connecting. The Network hosts church planter Connection Events in many regions across the United States, Mexico, and the Caribbean.

Number nine is the *Creativity* environment.

It's a new day for ministry isn't it? New paradigms are surfacing, like missional emphases, video venues, multi-site, post-modern, modern, classic, traditional, and next-gen ministries. We hear about the organic church, the simple church, the house church, the coffee house church, and at the same time we see the rise of the mega-church.

We're not here to force our favorite model on everyone, we just want to reach out and grow healthy churches. Jesus talked about "new wine." He was saying that innovation is necessary. If we insist on staying old and crusty and stuck in our ruts: "the skins will burst, the wine will run out and the wineskins will be ruined" (Matthew 9:17).

We are open to explore some of these "new wineskins." We're looking for Biblically-viable and practically-effective ways to start new congregations.

And tenth, we also offer a *Partnering* environment.

Some churches are ready to parent. Some aren't convinced they are even ready to babysit for half an hour. But everyone can do something in God's church planting movement. We've put together a network that offers a wide range of options for involvement – from giving a hundred people a hundred grand, to paying for that babysitter so the church planting couple can have some time to themselves.

This partnering piece also involves inviting leaders and team members to get involved in establishing and leading these environments.

And we are working diligently to foster partnerships with other networks, denominations, local judicatories, and churches.

The early church leaders turned the world upside down. They were filled with the Holy Spirit, committed to new leaders, set on keeping it simple, regularly meeting together, amazingly resilient, incredibly generous, extremely bold, and they had a clear strategy.

THE KEY QUESTION:

Which of the four parts of the Antioch Church strategy –
Spotting high-level leaders; setting leaders up for success;
sending out leaders; or supporting leaders – do you, your
church, or your network do best?

THE BIG CHALLENGE:

Identify by name, the high-level leaders connected
to your vision. Take time to consider how you are planning
to support them and set them up for success.

CHAPTER SIX

THE WHO

Alone we can do so little; together we can do so much.

—Helen Keller

The secret is to gang up on the problem, rather than each other.

—Thomas Stallkamp

Finding good players is easy. Getting them to play as a team is another story.

—Casey Stengel

In February of 1964, an up-and-coming rock group named "The Detours" consisting of Roger Daltrey, Pete Townshend and John Entwistle became aware of another band, known as Johnny Devlin and the Detours. So Daltrey, Townshend, and Entwistle needed a name change – quickly. They spent one night brainstorming ideas, centering on joke names like No One and The Group. By morning they had settled on The Who.

When it comes to church planting, who is the who? Who is the group that plants churches?

For years I've heard statements like, "Denominations don't start churches, churches start churches!" I've heard some churches say, "We don't start churches, we let our denomination do that." And I used to think,

"Denominations don't start churches, and churches don't start churches, church planters start churches."

It took me a couple decades to realize all of those statements aren't exactly correct.

Acts 13 outlines "the who" of church planting:

> In the church at Antioch there were prophets and teachers: Barnabas, Simeon called Niger, Lucius of Cyrene, Manaen (who had been brought up with Herod the tetrarch) and Saul. While they were worshiping the Lord and fasting, the Holy Spirit said, "Set apart for me Barnabas and Saul for the work to which I have called them." So after they had fasted and prayed, they placed their hands on them and sent them off.
>
> —Acts 13:1-3

I have seen too many churches start – stunningly – without God.

This passage suggests at least five members of the church planting "who."

1. God

It is God who starts churches. The idea for the mission comes from the Holy Spirit. If God ain't in it, ain't *nobody* in it!

Unfortunately, I have seen too many churches start – stunningly – without God. Many church splits that result in some sort of new church do so without the least bit of consideration toward God. I've heard planters admit that their primary motivation for planting consisted of showing their old dissuading pastor that they could "succeed." Some have as their big motive the need for a denominational church in the area. Some start a church based on what *not* to do (what their old pastor did), rather than on a vision of what *to* do. Some planters simply have a discontent, but it may not be what Bill Hybels calls, "that holy discontent."

We need to make sure that God is the primary partner and leader on the team.

2. The church planter

Acts 13 indicates that church planting is a team effort. In addition to God, we see Barnabas involved. Barnabas was the church planter. He was the earthly leader. Everything we read about him up to now showed that he was the skipper and Saul was the first mate.

The phrase, *"Barnabas and Saul"* is used eight times in the book of Acts before we see *"Paul and Barnabas"* used in Acts 13:15.

Church planters do plant churches. But sadly, I have seen several churches start without a church planter. A "core group" of folks may gather to begin a new church and then seek a leader to come and join them. This is one of the toughest ways to start a church. Often the planter who comes in realizes that someone else is the actual leader.

Our first church plant started this way. Five couples in their fifties had a vision to reach young families. They had been meeting for a while before they asked Lori and me to come and lead them. I was young and naïve. I didn't even realize that people who were older than me, and came before me, had to sacrifice to follow me. We immediately

Loneliness,
isolation,
and fatigue
become even
bigger issues
in church
plants that
are started
without a
team.

experienced a lot of growth and momentum, so those struggles got postponed in the process. But the struggles did come. Seven years later, Leroy, the natural leader in the group, confessed to me, "We wanted to see young people come to Jesus and get involved in ministry and we have seen our vision realized. And it is driving my wife and me crazy!"

3. The church planting team

The Holy Spirit in Acts 13 does not send the church planter out in a solo endeavor. It is "Barnabas and Saul" who are sent. This follows the pattern of Jesus who enlisted his followers and "sent them out two by two" (Acts 6:7 CEV, Luke 10:1 CEV).

Perhaps Jesus sent his disciples out two by two because of the Jewish tradition of two witnesses being necessary to solidify the truth. Maybe it was because of the strength in partnership.

> Two are better than one, because they have a good
> return for their labor: If either of them falls down,
> one can help the other up. But pity anyone who
> falls and has no one to help them up.
> —Ecclesiastes 4:9-10 (NIV)

Bob Logan, that great church planting guru and my first planting coach, wrote, "Forbes Magazine researched thousands of new businesses. They discovered that those that started with partners were four times more likely to succeed than those that started as solo entrepreneurs."

Most church plants begin without a church planting team. Typically it is simply the church planter leading. Loneliness, isolation, and fatigue become even bigger issues in church plants that are started without a team.

4. The sending church

The church in Antioch served as the "mother church" in Acts 13. They sent out two of their leaders along with John Mark a few verses later.

In their book *Leading Church Multiplication*, Tom Nebel and Steve Pike write:

> Multiple choice: is it best for children to grow up A) homeless and parentless on the streets B) in an orphanage or C) with their parents in a loving family? This is not a trick question, you can safely choose the obviously correct answer. Yes, it's with their parents in a loving family.[14]

Clearly having a parent church is the most ideal way to start new churches.

But most church plants do not have a mother church. When I was raising support for our second church plant, I used the line: "We don't have a mother church, but we're looking for all the aunts and uncles we can get – especially rich uncles!"

---

14   Tom Nebel and Steve Pike, *Leading Church Multiplication* (Churchsmart Resources, 2014).

Dave Ferguson reports that 96% of churches in America are not reproducing. If only 4% are reproducing, then a parenting church is a rarity.

5. The sending agency

We have already seen that the church in Antioch was closely tied to the church in Jerusalem. There was a partnership.

Barnabas and Saul were originally involved in the church in Jerusalem.

Acts 15 suggests some sort of network between the churches in Acts – Jerusalem, Antioch, Syria and Cilicia. So it wasn't just the Antioch church that sent out Barnabas and Saul. There is Biblical precedent for networks or denominations, or what Tom Nebel calls "a denominetwork."

So who is the who? God, the planter, the team, the sending church, and the agency.

Behind every great person…are a bunch of other people. Behind a church planting change…are a whole bunch of people, too.

Behind every great person ... are a bunch of other people. Behind a church planting change ... are a whole bunch of people, too.

I have found that church plants with more of these five ingredients tend to do much better than plants with less – obviously the aim would be to find as many of these partners as possible when we start new churches. But we are also aiming at church planters, teams, church planting churches, and church planting sending agencies to form a team to change things. If we allow God to take the lead, we as a team can change the church planting world.

THE KEY QUESTION:

How many of the team elements - God, the planter,
the team, the sending church, and the sending network -
were involved in the starting of your church?
How about in the last church you helped start?

THE BIG CHALLENGE:

Take this time to give your vision over to God, realizing that
He needs to be its source, its driving force, and its destination.

PART TWO:

CHANGING THE CHURCH

PLANTING WORLD

If you can really make a difference in just one
person's life...That's not enough.

Dennis Miller

Take out your mind every now and then and
dance on it, it's getting all caked up.

Vance Havner

Unless someone like you cares a whole awful lot,
nothing is going to get better. It's not.

Dr. Seuss

CHAPTER SEVEN

FROM ACCIDENTAL TO ACTS

The book of Acts alone is filled with stories of these seemingly ordinary people doing outrageous, extraordinary things.

—Aaron Tredway, *Outrageous: Awake to the Unexpected Adventures of Everyday Faith*

Intentional living is the art of making our own choices before others' choices make us.

—Richie Norton

When you live each day with intentionality, there's almost no limit to what you can do. You can transform yourself, your family, your community, and your nation. When enough people do that, they can change the world. When you intentionally use your everyday life to bring about positive change in the lives of others, you begin to live a life that matters.

—John C. Maxwell, *Intentional Living: Choosing a Life That Matters*

I spoke with the Executive Pastor, and then the Senior Pastor, of Purpose Church recently. They both told me how they had planted a daughter church from their large congregation and how they had three so-called satellites going, but they were quick to add, it was all accidental. Opportunistic situations dropped into their laps and they really didn't know what they were doing. It struck me as a bit funny that Purpose Church was repro-ducing but not on *purpose*. In their defense, the church changed its name to Purpose Church after its accidental planting. And now they are starting new churches on purpose.

So much of church planting in North America appears to be simply accidental, unplanned, and by chance. Stunningly, half of all church reproduction in North America is unintentional.

So much of everything we do in our culture tends to be unintentional.

> **Q:** How does a man show that he is planning
>   for the future?
> **A:** He buys two cases of beer.

We can be so unintentional.

Israel and Veronica were planting a church in Tijuana. It was going pretty well, they had a strong passion to reach children, and the new church was growing and had a vital children's ministry. Another couple in their organization was also planting a church at the time in Orange County, California. But that couple ran into immigration docu-mentation problems. They were going to be sent back to Mexico.

So the church planting organization came up with an opportunistic idea. They decided to make a trade. Israel and Veronica would become the pastors of the work in

Orange County, while the other couple would take over in Tijuana.

What could go wrong? Everything! And almost everything did. The group in Orange County never saw Israel and Veronica as their leaders and the work stalled. The other couple moved to Tijuana, didn't have much of a desire to help children, and both plants sputtered.

If someone had spent, say, five minutes thinking about the consequences, a great deal of hurt could have been prevented. Recently, Israel and Veronica were presented with the possi-

> **What could go wrong? Everything! And almost everything did.**

bility of leading another church start in Orange County. Their reply: "We're scared to death!"

Zig Ziglar quipped, "People don't tend to wander around and suddenly find themselves at the top of Mount Everest." We need to have a sense of intentionality and purpose.

Rick Weber, a leader in the North American Baptist Association says, unintentional church planting is often, "designed for disaster."

The Biblical writers clearly reveal a God of purpose. And in the Book of Acts we see amazing intentionality.

Three Models

As I read the Acts of the Apostles, I only see three models for extending God's kingdom. There's the Jerusalem method in Acts 8; the Antioch method in Acts 13; and the Corinthians method in Acts 18.

In Acts 8 we see *the Jerusalem method* for expansion:

> A great persecution broke out against the church in Jerusalem, and all except the apostles were scattered throughout Judea and Samaria.
>
> —Acts 8:1 (NIV)

Persecution is one strategy for church reproduction. Scattering because of suffering really works for outreach. Look at China or Cuba, those countries are experiencing significant revival due in large part to governmental oppression.

Persecution is one strategy for church reproduction. Scattering because of suffering really works for outreach.

Maybe we should simply pray, "God we really want to make an impact so will you please allow some sort of horrific, terrible tragedy and suffering to hit us. We are too complacent and set in our ways, so really let us have it God, so we will scatter and be forced into expanding your kingdom!"

I vote "No" on the Jerusalem method. If God wants to do that, he is God, so okay. But if I have a choice, I would like to pass.

In Acts 18 we see *the Corinthian method* for kingdom expansion:

> But when they opposed and insulted him, Paul shook the dust from his clothes and said, "Your blood is upon your own heads – I am innocent. From now on I will go preach to the Gentiles."
>
> —Acts 18:6 (NLT)

I am clear of my responsibility. From now on I will
go to the Gentiles.

—Acts 18:6 (NIV)

This is the Earl Weaver model. Earl Weaver was the
manager for baseball's Baltimore Orioles for many years
— so many years that for decades he held the record for
being thrown out of baseball games more than any other
manager or player. One time, he was asked by a reporter if
there was a trick to getting thrown out. Was there a magic
word or words that would automatically get him ejected?
And Weaver admitted, "One approach worked every time.
If I really wanted to get tossed, I would slowly stroll out
to the umpire. I'd look him in the eyes and simply ask,
'Are you going to get any better, or is this it?' That got me
ejected every single time."

This is the fig tree model. You're not doing anything?
Boom! May you never bear fruit again!

The Corinthian prayer is, "Dear God, we suck. We're
not doing a dang thing to reach people, so will you just
curse us, or better yet, just wipe us off the face of the earth?
Seriously, we're basically just in the way. So, smite us and
be done with it, in Jesus' name, Amen!"

Again, I vote "No!" I don't like option one or option
three.

I propose option two, *the Antioch method*.

Now in the church at Antioch there were prophets and teachers: Barnabas, Simeon called Niger,
Lucius of Cyrene, Manaen (who had been brought

up with Herod the tetrarch) and Saul. While they were worshiping the Lord and fasting, the Holy Spirit said, "Set apart for me Barnabas and Saul for the work to which I have called them." So after they had fasted and prayed, they placed their hands on them and sent them off.

—Acts 13:1-3 (NIV)

I recommend we intentionally, deliberately, thoughtfully, set apart and support high-level leaders.

When God says, "Set apart top leaders for the work I have for them," our response in America has not just been, "No," it's been, "Heck No!"

Now I don't know if the Antioch church raised any questions with God. I don't know if they pushed back and said, "But God, Barnabas and Saul? Barnabas is not only our pastor, he's our top giver. Saul is our youth pastor! We're in a building program. We're not large enough. The economy is suffering, the budget isn't stable enough, sending them off would be too expensive. And what about us? What about our needs?"

I don't know if they asked those questions. But I do know this. They didn't let those questions stop them from God's primary strategy for kingdom expansion – intentionally supporting high-level leaders.

Honestly, when God says, "Set apart top leaders for the work I have for them," our response in America has not just been, "No," it's been, "Heck No!" We've got programs to run and budgets to meet and our own kingdoms to perpetuate, we can't afford to set apart the Barnabas and Saul leaders in our churches. So, we've said, "No" to God.

What if we changed that "No" to a "Yes"? What if we turned things around so we were intentional about leadership development and kingdom reproduction?

It Was Good For Paul and Silas

You get the call. Or the dreaded email. You check your mail and the dubious letter is in it. The "we need to talk" message is received. Or it comes via text, Facebook, or a direct message on Twitter. It has happened to every pastor, every church planter, everyone in ministry. Someone is leaving the church. That couple you thought would always be there isn't going to be there anymore. The volunteer who was destined for, or even involved in, leadership is leaving your ministry. The solid folks aren't solid any longer. Maybe they had to move for job-related reasons, maybe they are mad at you and won't talk it out, maybe they are tired of talking it out, or maybe they are having a season of temporary insanity. Whatever, it is over. They are gone.

When people go, how do we keep going? When people leave, when good people – gifted people, our best people – exit, how do we keep on going?

The early church leaders lend some insight:

> Some time later Paul said to Barnabas, "Let us go back and visit the believers in all the towns where we preached the word of the Lord and see how they are doing." Barnabas wanted to take John, also called Mark, with them, but Paul did not think

it wise to take him, because he had deserted them in Pamphylia and had not continued with them in the work. They had such a sharp disagreement that they parted company. Barnabas took Mark and sailed for Cyprus, but Paul chose Silas and left, commended by the believers to the grace of the Lord. He went through Syria and Cilicia, strengthening the churches.

—Acts 15:36-41 (NIV)

Paul and Barnabas were the first church planters. They had to be the best of friends. They were ministry partners that saw many miracles and survived almost as many setbacks. But their partnership was over.

It must have been gut-wrenching. Can you imagine the hurt that both of these men must have felt? There had to be a good amount of confusion. This was a true crisis that could've hamstrung the early church. I'm sure there were tears.

But they separated.

And...

They kept going.

How did they keep going?

There's a phrase in this passage that I simply missed the first hundred or so times I read it. I have taught on this passage, preached on this passage, written about this passage, but I always missed this phrase:

...but Paul chose Silas and left...

—Acts 15:40 (NIV)

Paul chose Silas. Wait a minute. Who the flip is Silas? Silas had come on the scene eighteen verses earlier. Silas was mentioned with a man named Judas, also called Barsabbas. (Barsabbas means, "There's no way we're calling you Judas!") They were part of the Jerusalem church. They had emerged as leaders, prophets, and were chosen to be messengers to the church in Antioch.

> Here's the point: We always need to have a Silas ready. We must be intentional about leadership development.

Back to our question, how did Paul keep going even after his friend Barnabas left him? The answer is: Paul chose Silas.

Paul had a Silas to fall back on. Paul had a depth-chart full of leaders to help him. When Barnabas left and Mark left, Paul chose Silas.

Here's the point:

We always need to have a Silas ready. We must be intentional about leadership development.

If we have a Silas ready, we won't be as devastated when someone leaves the church. Sure it will hurt. But it won't demoralize us. It won't stop us.

If we have a Silas ready, we won't be so disappointed when one of our team members needs to move out of the area. We will be able to handle it as one of life's necessary endings.

If we have a Silas ready, we can stand our ground – even if it means someone may leave us.

If we have a Silas ready, we can make the tough call. We can fire the person who needs to be fired. Many churches are only one or two firings away from effectiveness. But we don't fire anyone because we don't have anyone ready to replace them.

If we have a Silas ready, we can leave when God tells us to leave.

If we have a Silas ready, we can see ministry reproduce rather than shrink.

If we have a Silas ready, we'll be in a position to take advantage of opportunities for expanding ministry.

We always need to have a Silas ready.

Guess what Paul did immediately after choosing Silas: The very next verse shows he added Timothy to the depth chart:

> Paul went first to Derbe and then to Lystra, where there was a young disciple named Timothy. His mother was a Jewish believer, but his father was a Greek. Timothy was well thought of by the believers in Lystra and Iconium, so Paul wanted him to join them on their journey.
>
> —Acts 16:1-3 (NLT)

Paul was consistently reproducing leaders!

So, how do we make sure we have a Silas and a Timothy ready? How can we be intentional about leadership development?

Sometimes we relax when we choose our number two person. But Paul had a number two, a number three, a number four...

1. Be on the lookout

Paul and Barnabas seemed to always be on the lookout for potential leaders. Barnabas found Saul and John Mark. Paul spotted Silas…and Timothy and Titus and Luke. I suspect there is a Silas in all of our lives – and a Barsabbas, too. Maybe we have to look back eighteen verses in our lives, but Silas might already be there.

2. Give second chances

This is what the argument was all about. John Mark had flaked out once, but Barnabas didn't give up. He gave John Mark a second chance – and it paid off. Paul later wrote to Timothy, "Get Mark and bring him with you, because he is helpful to me in my ministry" (2 Timothy 4:11 NIV).

3. Never stop recruiting and developing

Sometimes we relax when we choose our number two person. But Paul had a number two, a number three, a number four…recruitment and development never end. I need to remind myself, and the leaders around me, that we're always looking for the next leader, the next servant, the next Silas.

4. Change my perspective

Paul didn't see his role as one of building his kingdom or even having a team that would be together forever. His goal was kingdom expansion and his role included leadership development. I need to make sure I have that same perspective.

People may leave my church. Some who I thought were on board may jump ship. Things will change. But I need to keep going, to think kingdom, and to always be on the lookout for the next leader to develop.

If it was good for Paul and Silas, it's good enough for me.

Shrewd as Snakes

Jesus told us to be "as shrewd as snakes..." (Matthew 10:16 NLT).

He added, "And it is true that the children of this world are more shrewd in dealing with the world around them than are the children of the light" (Luke 16:8 NLT).

Shrewdness, intentionality, and wisdom should mark our decisions. We're to be as wise as snakes.

I recently looked into why snakes are considered to be wise. The results startled me. There were no studies showing snakes to be all that intelligent. Snakes are not known for being smart – although one python recently was able to open a door. How about that for a creepy thought?

Snakes' shrewdness is seen in that they know when to move; they know when to hide; and they know when to strike.

A synonym for shrewd is prudent, and the wisest man outside of Jesus, King Solomon, said:

> The prudent see danger and take refuge, but the simple keep going and suffer for it.
>
> —Proverbs 27:12 (NIV)

and:

> The wisdom of the prudent is to give thought to their ways.
>
> —Proverbs 14:8 NIV)

It is time to be shrewd. It is time to strike – to change the church planting world with intentionality.

THE KEY QUESTION:

When it comes to leadership development,
how intentional am I?

THE BIG CHALLENGE:

Move to the Antioch Method by identifying the
Barnabases and Sauls and Silases in your midst.

CHAPTER EIGHT

FROM HYPE TO HOLY SPIRIT

Care more for a grain of faith than a ton of excitement.

—Charles Spurgeon

The greatest need of the church today is more of the presence and power of the Spirit of God.

—Dwight L. Moody

It's a temptation that exists for everyone - for talk and hype to replace action.

—Ryan Holiday, *Ego is the Enemy*

A college recruiter heard great things about a high-school basketball player from a small town. The recruiter arrived too late to see the player's game, but he met the young man and said, "I hear you're pretty good."

"The best there is," the player replied. "I average 45 points a game, I lead the team in rebounds and assists, and because of me we've won three straight state titles."

"Wow," the recruiter said. Then he turned to the coach and asked, "With all that talent, does he have any weaknesses?"

The coach said sheepishly, "He does have a tendency to exaggerate."

The great and powerful Wizard of Oz uttered that iconic line, "Pay no attention to that man behind the curtain." The wizard revealed that hype isn't always healthy. Sometimes the hoopla masks reality.

The hype surrounding church planting these days is startling. When my wife and I started our first church back in 1983, there were very few materials available about starting churches. I found a small binder put together by a serial planter named Len Waterman, but that was it.

Today, propaganda for planting seems to be everywhere.

Ed Stetzer writes:

> There's no question that church planting has become the hot new thing. And I'm glad. When I started my first church in 1988, it was an oddity. Now, it is mainstream…

> Books, conferences, and initiatives that champion church planting are manifold. This is a good thing. But it seems to me we've got better conferences and bigger excitement and, according to the research, only incremental progress when it comes to the evangelistic fruits of actual church planting. Statistically, we have more church planting, but slightly less evangelistic impact. And, most importantly, too many church plants don't have the needed evangelistic focus that should undergird what they do.

Planting should be a viable option that many ministers look into. But there are big problems with church planting hype.

Planting is now the sexy ministry. The sense is that all one needs is a cool haircut, some sort of facial hair, skinny jeans, and the church planter purse (carryall, man-bag, satchel, man-purse, "murse") for a church of a thousand to emerge.

Certainly some of this publicity for entrepreneurial ministry is great. Planting should be a viable option that many ministers look into. But there are big problems with church planting hype.

First, *the hype can cause too many people not called to plant to go out and plant.*

Not everyone is called to be a church planter. Perhaps we need conferences where there is an altar call for those not called to start a church to come forward. The Holy Spirit said that Barnabas and Paul should go, but doesn't that mean the Holy Spirit implied that Simeon, Lucius and Manaen were called to not go?

Maybe the advertising, the excitement, and the constant barrage of emails from some organizations doesn't necessarily mean we all should do this.

Second, *the hype can communicate church planting is easy.*

Hall of Fame football coach Lou Holtz warns, "If you do not make a total commitment to whatever you are doing, then you start looking to bail out the first time the boat starts leaking. It is tough enough getting that boat to shore with everybody rowing, let alone when a guy stands up and starts putting his life jacket on."

Third, and maybe most importantly, *the hype can be so noisy that we don't hear the most important voice.*

In Acts 13, the Holy Spirit spoke. The most important phrase of that entire passage is arguably: "The Holy Spirit said…" (Acts 13:2 NIV).

God's voice was pretty active in those days. A couple chapters earlier we read where Peter's desire to reach out to non-Jews came from:

> Soon the news reached the apostles and other believers in Judea that the Gentiles had received the word of God. But when Peter arrived back in Jerusalem, the Jewish believers criticized him. "You entered the home of Gentiles and even ate with them!" they said. Then Peter told them exactly what had happened…
> —Acts 11:1-4 (NLT)

When the news reached the church leaders in Jerusalem that something new had started, that a different kind of people were turning to God, the leaders immediate response was to criticize the instigator – Peter.

But Peter didn't allow criticism to stop him. Peter pushed through the disparagement with an explanation. He told them exactly what happened. He explained how the Holy Spirit spoke clearly several times. Then he summed it up:

> So if God gave them the same gift he gave us who believed in the Lord Jesus Christ, who was I to think that I could stand in God's way?
> —Acts 11:17 (NIV)

For church planting to happen, someone needs to have an encounter with the Holy Spirit.

Peter's encounter was contagious: "When the others heard this, they stopped objecting and began praising God" (Acts 11:18 NLT).

Peter had an encounter with the Holy Spirit and then the other leaders had a similar encounter.

Church planting is God's idea. But church planting is often stopped in its tracks because no one has had an interaction with the Holy Spirit.

Senior pastors stop any talk of church planting through their church because they haven't heard the Holy Spirit. Boards nix planting because they haven't heard the Holy Spirit speak. Denominations put planting on the back burner or off the burner completely — because they haven't heard anything from God.

> **Church planting is often stopped in its tracks because no one has had an interaction with the Holy Spirit.**

How do you counteract that? We can't schedule the Holy Spirit to speak. We can't make God talk to our leaders. We can't orchestrate encounters with the Holy Spirit.

But I believe there is something we *can* do. I'm not condoning manipulation or some spiritual misapplication. But if we look at Acts chapter 13 we do see something that the leaders did that seemingly sparked the Holy Spirit to speak:

> While they were worshiping the Lord and fasting, the Holy Spirit said…
>
> —Acts 13:2 (NIV)

The Holy Spirit spoke when they worshiped and fasted.

We see it again in the next verse:

> So after they had fasted and prayed, they placed
> their hands on them and sent them off.
> —Acts 13:3 (NIV)

When they fasted they heard the Holy Spirit speak. But they didn't act immediately, they fasted again, just to make sure they were hearing correctly, before sending off Barnabas and Saul.

Running On Empty

It actually happened to me once. When I was a student at UCLA, I often spent the night at my sister's house in Manhattan Beach. On one of those occasions, I got up super early to make my shift stocking shelves at the Ralph's grocery store in Century City before going to class. Driving north on the surprisingly traffic-free 405, a Jackson Browne song was blasting on the radio when the memorable event took place: I ran out of gas to the tune of "Running on Empty."

> *Running on empty, running blind,*
> *looking into the sun but I'm running behind.*
> —Jackson Browne

Running on empty is something I've done a lot of in my life. One of my college friends told me it took him a while to face the fact that if he was going to ride in my car he needed to accept that I didn't mind running out of gas. I asked him how many times I ran out of gas with him in my car. He said, "Let's just say more than once."

I've been financially challenged, paying my way through college, graduate school, starting churches, having kids – for years I didn't want to die with too much gas in the car (that would be poor stewardship!). Pushing an old beater, or taking a walk with a gas can is good exercise.

Years ago, I bought my wife, Lori, a 1966 Mustang coupe for her birthday. It's a great car, but we have never been able to get the gas gauge to work. I cannot tell you the number of times we ran out of gas in that car – AAA might have a record. It's simple math, fill it up, add 175 miles and re-fuel before you hit that number on the odometer. We still managed to be running on empty and running blind.

We don't drive that car anymore. Actually it's for sale! (Make me an offer!) We've matured. I've grown to the point where I realize I don't need the stress or the angst of running down the road on empty.

I still slip into running on empty in other ways though. Physically, sometimes I push it too hard, travel too much, and sleep too little. Financially, we've set up our emergency fund so we're not facing *too much month* with *too little money* too often. But it still happens every once in a while. Relationally, I can get disconnected from friends, family, even my wife if I'm not intentional about it.

And spiritually, I think a lot of us end up running on empty.

Jackson Browne may have been on to it when he wrote:

Everyone I know, everywhere I go
People need some reason to believe
I don't know about anyone but me...

Looking out at the road rushing under my wheels
I don't know how to tell you all just how crazy this
life feels
I look around for the friends that I used to turn to
pull me through
Looking into their eyes I see them running too

Are you running on empty?

Most of us really want to do what we were meant to do spiritually. We were made for a purpose. We were created to influence the people that God has strategically, sovereignly, even supernaturally put into our lives.

Most of us really want to do what we were meant to do spiritually. But a lot of us are just exhausted.

But a lot of us are just exhausted. Life gets crazy. Work, marriage, kids, kids' activities, kids' sports, there's political issues I'm trying to keep up on, extended family stuff, and if there is ever a crisis, or even a mini-crisis, we catch ourselves running on empty.

How can we keep from running out of gas?

One story from the life and teaching of Jesus gives us an idea. In Mark chapter 9, Jesus had just taken Peter, James, and John up on a mountain where he was transfigured – this was a picture of heaven with Jesus, Moses, and

Elijah. It was an incredible spiritual high, a vision of the future, a powerful moment. They came down the mountain and ran into powerlessness.

> As they approached the other disciples, they saw a large crowd around them and some scribes arguing with them. The whole crowd was very surprised to see Jesus and ran to welcome him.

> He asked the scribes, "What are you arguing about with them?" A man in the crowd answered him, "Teacher, I brought my son to you. He has a spirit that won't let him talk. Whenever it brings on a seizure, it throws him to the ground. Then he foams at the mouth, grinds his teeth, and becomes stiff. So I asked your disciples to drive the spirit out, but they didn't have the power."
> —Mark 9:14-18 (ISV)

Jesus' disciples didn't appear to have the power. They were running on empty. And this obviously annoyed Jesus.

> Jesus told them, "You unbelieving generation! How long must I be with you? How long must I put up with you? Bring him to me!"
> —Mark 9:19 (ISV)

Jesus had just experienced heaven, and then he came to earth only to see his disciples in the midst of a failure.

So they brought the boy to him. When the spirit saw Jesus, it immediately threw the boy into convulsions. He fell on the ground and kept rolling around and foaming at the mouth. Then Jesus asked his father, "How long has this been happening to him?" He said, "Since he was a child. The spirit has often thrown him into fire and into water to destroy him. But if you are able to do anything, have pity on us and help us!" Jesus told him, "'If you are able?'"

—Mark 9:20-23 (ISV)

Again Jesus seems perturbed. "If you are able?" Are you kidding me? It is almost as if he is saying, "Casting out demons is beginner work. My disciples should have been able to handle this kids' stuff!"

Jesus told him, "Everything is possible for the person who believes!" With tears flowing, the child's father at once cried out, "I do believe! Help my unbelief!"

—Mark 9:23-24 (ISV)

When Jesus saw that a crowd was running to the scene, he rebuked the unclean spirit, saying to it, "You spirit that won't let him talk or hear – I command you to come out of him and never enter him again!" The spirit screamed, shook the child violently, and came out. The boy was like a corpse, and many said that he was dead. But Jesus took his hand and helped him up, and he stood up.

—Mark 9:25-27

The disciples can't perform the exorcism, so Jesus steps in and immediately cures the boy.

> When Jesus came home, his disciples asked him privately, "Why couldn't we drive the spirit out?"
>
> —Mark 9:28

Great question: Why didn't we have the power? Why were we so empty? How do we make sure this doesn't happen again? Jesus gives a surprising answer:

> He told them, "This kind can come out only by prayer and fasting."
>
> —Mark 9:14-29 (ISV)

Jesus concludes that the key to tapping into His power is prayer and fasting.

The way to never be empty is to empty ourselves. That is so counter-intuitive. We are never empty if we empty ourselves. We need to be prayed up and fasted up in order to be filled up.

Prayer is powerful.

> The prayer of a person living right with God is something powerful to be reckoned with.
>
> —James 5:16 (MSG)

Fasting is powerful.
Dan Allendar put it this way:

Fasting from any nourishment, activity, involvement or pursuit—for any season—sets the stage for God to appear. Fasting is not a tool to pry wisdom out of God's hands or to force needed insight about a decision. Fasting is not a tool for gaining discipline or developing piety (whatever that might be). Instead, fasting is the bulimic act of ridding ourselves of our fullness to attune our senses to the mysteries that swirl in and around us.

One prescription to fill up our spiritual tanks involves prayer and fasting.

I think we get tripped up on this. Many of us have been led to believe that we have to pray for an hour every day in order for it to count. So, we rarely pray. It seems like too much. But check this out. How long does "The Lord's Prayer" take? Maybe a minute…When Jesus was asked by his followers, "Teach us to pray…" he started with a one-minute prayer.

Pray for an hour if you'd like, pray all night sometimes. But start with a minute, or two, or five.

What about fasting? How long should we fast? One of our roadblocks is the first example we think of is Jesus fasting forty days and forty nights. That's beyond the reach of…just about everyone. And Jesus only did that one time that we know of. Twenty-five times the Bible mentions fasting, and only once was it for forty days.

How about starting by fasting for a meal? Or dessert? Or a snack?

Last year I decided to get intentional about it. I've made a commitment, and I'm asking the people on our leadership team, advisory team, all the church planters, and every supporter in our network to fast and pray during one meal a week seeking the Holy Spirit to show up in our network.

Fast one meal per week. Anybody can do that. I have found that you can actually gain weight fasting! My goal this year was to lose ten pounds, only fifteen more to go!

I ran out of gas to the song "Running on Empty." I was actually able to coast off of the freeway right into a gas station. I remember pumping the gas with a huge smile on my face.

When we run out of gas spiritually it isn't always without consequences. Maybe others are counting on us – like the poor man coming to the disciples with his troubled son. If I'm out of gas it might mean bad news for myself and others, so I need to get – and stay – filled up.

The good news is, when we run out of gas spiritually, God has a filling station that we can coast into no matter where we are. He's available and He wants to fill us up.

THE KEY QUESTION:

Who am I listening to? Where does God's voice
appear on my list?

THE BIG CHALLENGE:

Start fasting one meal per week for church planting. As you fast, ask the Holy Spirit to show up for you and your ministry.

CHAPTER NINE

FROM INSTITUTION TO LEADER

Leaders are like eagles...they don't flock. You'll find them one at a time.

—Knute Rockne

I've searched all the parks in all the cities and found no statues of committees.

—G. K. Chesterton

The Church is looking for better methods; God is looking for better men.

—E.M. Bounds

Seth Godin asks a pretty interesting question. "What are corporations for?"
Then he adds:

> Somewhere along the way, people got the idea that maximizing investor return was the point. It shouldn't be. The great corporations of a generation ago, the ones that built key elements of our culture, were run by individuals who had more on their mind than driving the value of their options up. Profits and stock price aren't the point (with customers as a side project). It's the other way around.

Denominations can slip into similar thinking. I suspect the great denominations of the past, the ones that built key elements of our culture, were run by individuals who had more on their mind than driving the value of their options up.

For most denominations, most of the time, their primary customer is themselves.

Financial guru David Bennett told me of a recent conversation he had with an insurance salesperson he was coaching. "How can I get people interested in my product?" the salesperson asked. "All they seem to care about is themselves." David said his first thought was, "Hello, McFly!" Then he answered, "That is the point! Find out what people care about, and either fit your product to help them, or send them to someone who will." Then David suggested this simple approach: "The most overlooked fund-raising principle isn't that planters need a better 'pitch'. They'd get better fund raising results if they would take the prospective donor out for lunch, ask questions, and shut up."

For most denominations, most of the time, their primary customer is themselves. You hear it in their vision, "We are here to help our churches. We need to protect the integrity of our tribe." When the denomination sent their third-string-accountant to our church planting meetings in Phoenix, they were just doing what many denominations do, they were looking out for themselves. They wanted us to help them save their denomination.

Michael Smith remarked, "As an organization gets larger there can be a tendency for the 'institution' to dampen the 'inspiration.'"

Churches also tend to digress so that their primary customer is themselves. Decisions are made on "preserving our church" rather than furthering the message. We easily get more interested in what is happening inside our walls, than the mission outside our walls.

Carey Nieuwhof observed in his book, *Lasting Impact*:

> Typically, people change when the pain associated with the status quo becomes greater than the pain associated with change. In many churches, as long as the bills are being paid and people are still showing up, the motivation to change remains too low to really push ahead...[15]

Notice in Acts 13, the Holy Spirit revealed the primary customer of the Antioch church:

> Set apart for me Barnabas and Saul for the work to which I have called them.
>
> —Acts 13:2

The primary focus was on leadership. Now, obviously God is our primary customer, and we're here to reach the lost. But as an institution, we do well to focus on leaders.

We must help change the focus from the organization as the primary customer to the leader as the primary customer.

---

15 Carey Nieuwhof, *Lasting Impact: 7 Powerful Conversations That Will Help Your Church Grow* (The rethink Group, Inc., 2016).

When we focus on the denomination or the individual church we become more and more ingrown. But if we focus on the leaders, the church tends to do just fine, and the denomination tends to do just fine as well.

One of my primary goals in life is to help move organizations from seeing their institution as the customer to seeing the leader as their responsibility.

Here is the key question we need to ask of those we support: "What can I do for you?"

Ken Blanchard says:

Here is the key question we need to ask of those we support: "What can I do for you?"

> All the great companies I know think their number one customer is their people. They think that if they take care of their people, motivate their people, train their people, they are going to go out of their way to take care of their number two customer, which is the people who use your products and services. When they do that they create raving fans from them, and that takes care of the people who own the company and the profitability. It all comes from the philosophy that profit is the applause you get for creating a motivating environment for your people who take care of your customers…You've got to realize that your people are your greatest asset, and when that is true, wow, they will take care of your customers.

When I started consulting in 2001, I wanted the church to be better. But since then my passion shifted. Today I want pastors to be freer. Specifically, I hope pastors feel freer, confident of what God is calling them to do, and, as a result, accomplishing more with their short lives on the earth.[16]

—Will Mancini and Warren Bird

The Cardinal Rule

When I left my previous organization I expected to be the target of backlash. But I was surprised when I heard that one church planter in that association, a friend I had coached for years, was publicly talking me down.

A few folks had told me that he had been going after me, so I let him know I would be in his city soon, and hoped we could get together. He said he couldn't. A few weeks later I was again going through his town and I suggested we get together. Again he said he couldn't meet. A third time I was scheduled to be in his area so I asked for a meeting. There was no response.

I asked my wife and my coach how many times I needed to try to get together with him, and they both said that three times would suffice, so I was off the hook. I do remember someone else saying something about seventy times seven times though...

The night before I was headed to my friend's town, I received a text. He said he'd meet me. After exchanging pleasantries, I mentioned that I'd heard from a few people that he had been saying some bad things about me

---

16   Will Mancini and Warren Bird, *God Dreams: 12 Vision Templates for Finding and Focusing Your Church's Future* (B&H Books, 2016).

publicly, so I wanted to talk to him to see what actually was happening.

"Oh, you're doing Matthew 18 on me, huh?" he asked. Then he clearly denied that he had spoken to anyone about me, before launching into a list of griev-ances he'd had against me for a long time. He vented, and I sensed that all of his angst could be whittled down to three issues.

> I realized that I had broken the cardinal rule of ministry: I violated the central purpose for church planting directors.

The first issue was he felt that I had taken the organization's side against him in a facility dispute. He was right. I apolo-gized. As the Church Planting Director my primary role was to serve him, and I had messed that up. Regardless of who I felt was right, my obligation needed to be to support him. He accepted my apology.

The third issue had to do with him saying I said some-thing that I certainly never said. I suspect it stemmed from his anger towards me on issue one and issue two. I plainly let him know I never said what he thought I'd said.

The second issue was the main culprit. He told me that when he had reached the last of his church planting milestones, I commented to him something along the lines of, "I never thought you would do it."

Now, I do not recollect ever saying that, and I do not recall ever even thinking anything of the sort – I definitely believed in this planter. I agreed to coach him. I could imagine that I may have joked about something like that. My warped sense of humor and desire for a laugh gets me in trouble more often than I'd like to admit. I apologized

profusely. If I communicated anything like that, I could understand
why he would have a problem with
me. I was truly sorry, and I believe
he forgave me.

As I drove away from that meeting I realized that I had broken the
cardinal rule of ministry: I violated the central purpose for
church planting directors.

**The Cardinal Rule
of Leadership is:
*Believe in your
people.* This rule
probably also
applies to parenting,
marriage, and
friendship.**

That rule is stated clearly by the Apostle Paul in the
book of Philippians. Paul's letter to the church in Philippi
outlines how leaders should operate.

> I am writing to all of God's holy people in Philippi
> who belong to Christ Jesus, including the church
> leaders and deacons.
>
> —Philippians 1:1 (NIV)

I think it is comical that Paul reminds his writers that
the church leaders actually belong to Jesus too!

And Paul states the cardinal rule for leaders in verse 6
of chapter 1:

> For I am confident of this very thing, that He who
> began a good work in you will perfect it until the
> day of Christ Jesus.
>
> —Philippians 1:6 (NASB)

Paul believed in the Philippians. He believed in the
leaders.

The Cardinal Rule of Leadership is: *Believe in your people.* This rule probably also applies to parenting, marriage, and friendship.

Charles Schwab observed, "I have yet to find the man, however exalted his station, who did not do better work and put forth greater effort under a spirit of approval than under a spirit of criticism."

The best bosses share a common characteristic: they are encouragers. It's easy to "…find the holes in someone's professional ability, but good bosses see a flicker of something and just let it barge out the front door."[17]

So how did the Apostle Paul come to be someone who believed in people?

First, *Paul experienced the impact of believing in people personally.* He was the recipient of someone believing in him.

> When Saul arrived in Jerusalem, he tried to meet with the believers, but they were all afraid of him. They did not believe he had truly become a believer! Then Barnabas brought him to the apostles and told them how Saul had seen the Lord on the way to Damascus and how the Lord had spoken to Saul. He also told them that Saul had preached boldly in the name of Jesus in Damascus.
>
> —Acts 9:26-27 (NLT)

---

17   Jason Gay, *Little Victories: Perfect Rules for Imperfect Living* (Knopf Doubleday Publishing Group, 2015), Kindle Edition.

Paul had firsthand experience of someone believing in him. The Jerusalem believers literally didn't believe him or believe in him.

Paul was a believer-killer. And when he turned to the Lord, I suspect that many people – most maybe – wrote him off. But Barnabas didn't. He saw the potential in Paul. Barnabas stood up for him. Barnabas vouched for him. And that changed his world.

This apparently insignificant little story about two men has actually impacted the entire world. Saul tracked down followers of Jesus and saw that they were killed. He was a borderline murderer. But then he had an encounter with Jesus – like many of us have experienced, and like many of us are seeking. He turned his life over to Jesus, but the believers were not immediately convinced. They didn't buy into his conversion, and most of them hoped he would go to church somewhere else.

But along came Barnabas. Barnabas decided to be an encourager, to spur Saul on until Saul became the Apostle Paul, a major player in the Christian movement, writer of nearly half the New Testament, and someone whose influence is still seen today.

A little encouragement goes a long way.

Michelle Pfeiffer admits, "I had a high school teacher who said one simple thing to me, 'I think you have talent.' And I never forgot it, partly because while growing up, I got very few compliments. Now, I didn't at that moment think, 'Oh, I'll be an actress.' Still, I came to feel very confident in that world because of that single comment."

> So Saul stayed with the apostles and went all around
> Jerusalem with them, preaching boldly in the name
> of the Lord.
>
> —Acts 9:28 (NLT)

Barnabas changed Paul's world, and we can change the
world of others if we simply believe in them.

Second, *Paul experienced believing in people corporately*.

> When the church at Jerusalem heard what had
> happened, they sent Barnabas to Antioch. When
> he arrived and saw this evidence of God's bless-
> ing, he was filled with joy, and he encouraged the
> believers to stay true to the Lord. Barnabas was
> a good man, full of the Holy Spirit and strong
> in faith. And many people were brought to the
> Lord.
>
> —Acts 11:22-24 (NLT)

Word of a newly forming church reached Jerusalem,
so they sent Barnabas – what an amazingly wise decision.

> Then Barnabas went on to Tarsus to look for Saul.
> When he found him, he brought him back to
> Antioch. Both of them stayed there with the church
> for a full year, teaching large crowds of people. (It
> was at Antioch that the believers were first called
> Christians.)
>
> —Acts 11:25-26 (NLT)

Paul got a front row seat to see what believing in people could do. The Antioch church was energized and propelled by Barnabas' encouragement. And Paul got to experience it.

But there's a third reason why Paul was so big on believing in people: *Paul experienced the impact of not believing in people.*

> After some time, Paul said to Barnabas, "Let's go back and visit each city where we previously preached the word of the Lord, to see how the new believers are doing." Barnabas agreed and wanted to take along John Mark. But Paul disagreed strongly, since John Mark had deserted them in Pamphylia and had not continued with them in their work. Their disagreement was so sharp that they separated.
>
> —Acts 15:36-39 (NLT)

Paul and Barnabas had agreed on a mission, but a disagreement, a sharp one, arose between them over John Mark. Barnabas believed in John Mark, Paul didn't, he saw John Mark as a deserter. And Paul didn't back down.

Perhaps Paul understood from his previous encounters that believing in people pays better dividends than not believing in people.

Can you imagine how difficult this break-up must have been? The Holy Spirit called them as a team, but a decision on whether or not to believe in a potential leader broke up the team. The author of Acts doesn't tell us who was right or wrong in the separation, but it isn't too far of a leap to suggest Paul may have regretted his move.

Later, Paul wrote this:

> Bring Mark with you when you come, for he will be helpful to me in my ministry.
> —2 Timothy 4:11 (NLT)

Perhaps Paul understood from his previous encounters that believing in people pays better dividends than not believing in people.

How Can We Believe?

So, how do we believe in others? How do we focus on the leaders? How do we move from institution-centered to leader-centered?

Let's look at the life of Paul and the books of Acts and Philippians for some practical suggestions.

1. Choose Wisely.

Paul mentions the "partnership" he has with the Philippian church people.

> …you have been my partners…
> —Philippians 1:5 (NLT)

> So it is right that I should feel as I do about all of you, for you have a special place in my heart.
> —Philippians 1:7 (NLT)

> We are in this struggle together. You have seen my
> struggle in the past, and you know that I am still in
> the midst of it.
>
> —Philippians 1:30 (NLT)

We need to make the best possible choices when it comes to who is partnering with us. Many denominations have turned inward because they have had bad experiences with renegade pastors in their tribe, or they do not really trust the pastors and leaders in their midst to show loyalty to the organization. Sometimes this lack of trust causes denominations to disenfranchise planters, pastors, and leaders without the denomination even realizing it.

Let me ask you a question, who are you partnering with?

Zig Ziglar preached, "Life is too short to spend your precious time trying to convince a person who wants to live in gloom and doom otherwise. Give lifting that person your best shot, but don't hang around long enough for his or her bad attitude to pull you down. Instead, surround yourself with optimistic people."

Choose wisely. I know this is difficult because our culture typically encourages us away from choosing to simply settling for our friends. We don't learn good friend-forming habits. We look at the kid sitting next to us in first-grade and we're stuck with him or her as our best friend until we graduate high school. The proverbial friendless American male got that way because he never learned to look past the next door neighbor or cubicle buddy for a pal.

The righteous choose their friends carefully, but the way of the wicked leads them astray.
—Proverbs 12:26 (NIV)

Walk with the wise and become wise; associate with fools and get in trouble.
—Proverbs 13:20 (NLT)

Do not be misled: "Bad company corrupts good character."
—1 Corinthians 15:33 (NIV)

Choose friends, leaders and partners shrewdly.

2. Think Regularly

Every time I think of you, I give thanks to my God.
—Philippians 1:3 (NLT)

One of the keys to leadership is thinking!

I have a friend in his sixties who works as a tour guide. He has been doing this sort of work for years. I suspect it doesn't pay that well, so I always wondered about why he chose that vocation. Then I took him out for a Coke and he told me his story: "I always wanted to be an actor," he confessed. Then his eyes lit up. "And I am! I get paid full-time to act every single day!"

My entire picture of my friend changed in that moment. He isn't a tour guide; he is a success.

> Fix your thoughts on what is true, and honorable,
> and right, and pure, and lovely, and admirable. Think
> about things that are excellent and worthy of praise.
> —Philippians 4:8 (NLT)

To believe in people we need to stop and think about them – their strengths, their gifts, their future – the good things.

Too often we spend so much time thinking about ourselves and our organizations, we miss that other people have so much to offer.

Paul Mints says, "For so many leaders, the way we've been building the kingdom…is destroying the kingdom inside of us. When people become a means to an end, we've lost the heart and mindset of Christ. There's a difference between a relationally-focused ministry approach and a program/event driven approach. We say it like this: 'YOU are more important than what you DO.'"

3. Thank Intentionally

> Every time I think of you, I give thanks to my God.
> —Philippians 1:3 (NLT)

> Don't worry about anything; instead, pray about
> everything. Tell God what you need, and thank
> him for all he has done.
> —Philippians 4:6 (NLT)

Paul is writing to the church in Philippi; he had planted that church. He's now in prison in Rome and he's writing with thanksgiving. Paul is thanking God for the people, and he is thanking them for financial gifts that they've given him, he's thanking them for their prayers, their support, for their love.

The longer we know someone, the easier it is to take them for granted. But if we are thoughtful, if we are intentionally thankful, we will see that it isn't that difficult to believe in other people.

4. Pray Consistently

> Whenever I pray, I make my requests for all of you
> with joy.
> —Philippians 1:4 (NLT)

Jeremy McGarity says, "Maybe you have a strained relationship with someone or they just rub you the wrong way. I have a question for you: Do you pray for them? Or do you just complain and grumble and nag and nitpick? If you'd pray more you'd have a lot less to grumble, complain, nag, and nitpick about."

Here is a sample of how to pray for people from Paul's prayer journal:

> I pray that your love will overflow more and more, and that you will keep on growing in knowledge and understanding. For I want you to understand what really matters, so that you may live pure and blameless lives until the day of Christ's return. May you always be filled with the fruit of your salvation

– the righteous character produced in your life by
Jesus Christ – for this will bring much glory and
praise to God.

—Philippians 1:9-11 (NLT)

5. Encourage Humbly

Is there any encouragement from belonging to
Christ? Any comfort from his love? Any fellow-
ship together in the Spirit? Are your hearts tender
and compassionate? Then make me truly happy by
agreeing wholeheartedly with each other, loving
one another, and working together with one mind
and purpose. Don't be selfish; don't try to impress
others. Be humble, thinking of others as better
than yourselves. Don't look out only for your own
interests, but take an interest in others, too. You
must have the same attitude that Christ Jesus had.
Though he was God, he did not think of equality
with God as something to cling to. Instead, he
gave up his divine privileges; he took the humble
position of a slave and was born as a human being.

—Philippians 2:1-7 (NLT)

It is very difficult to believe in people when I'm in an
arrogant, superior, egotistical state.

C.S. Lewis wrote in *Mere Christianity*, "If anyone
would like to acquire humility, I can, I think, tell him the
first step. The first step is to realize that one is proud. And
a biggish step, too. At least, nothing whatever can be done

before it. If you think you are not conceited, it means you are very conceited indeed."[18]

When we deal with our own pride, we can encourage others to be their best.

6. Address those we are struggling to believe in

As the Apostle Paul was writing about believing in people, he pivoted toward dealing with those we don't believe in. He was realistic enough to know that we may not end up believing in everyone.

Three Options in Dealing with People We Don't Believe in

A. Remove them immediately

Some people need to be out-counseled immediately. Look at these severe words:

> Don't be intimidated in any way by your enemies. This will be a sign to them that they are going to be destroyed, but that you are going to be saved, even by God himself.
>
> —Philippians 1:28 (NLT)

> Watch out for those dogs, those people who do evil, those mutilators who say you must be circumcised to be saved.
>
> —Philippians 3:2 (NLT)

---

18   C.S. Lewis, *Mere Christianity* (HarperOne, 2015).

For I have told you often before, and I say it again with tears in my eyes, that there are many whose conduct shows they are really enemies of the cross of Christ. They are headed for destruction. Their god is their appetite, they brag about shameful things, and they think only about this life here on earth.

—Philippians 3:18-29 (NLT)

Some people need to be pushed out of our lives immediately. Henry Cloud, in *Necessary Endings*, talks about evil people who may need to be handled by "lawyers, guns, and money."[19]

B. Don't Worry About Them

Others cause us trouble, but Paul seems to be able to set them aside.

It's true that some are preaching out of jealousy and rivalry. But others preach about Christ with pure motives. They preach because they love me, for they know I have been appointed to defend the Good News. Those others do not have pure motives as they preach about Christ. They preach with selfish ambition, not sincerely, intending to make my chains more painful to me. But that doesn't matter. Whether their motives are false or genuine, the message about Christ is being preached either way, so I rejoice.

—Philippians 1:15-18 (NLT)

---

19   Henry Cloud, *Necessary Endings* (HarperBusiness, 2011).

Did you catch Paul's response to other people's selfishness? "That doesn't matter..." Some people we can simply ignore. We can stop giving them so much power in our lives.

C. Connect Them to a Different Leader

A third group of folks who we may be struggling with can be dealt with like Paul treated John Mark:

> Their disagreement was so sharp that they separated. Barnabas took John Mark with him and sailed for Cyprus. Paul chose Silas, and as he left, the believers entrusted him to the Lord's gracious care.
>
> —Acts 15:39-40 (NLT)

Notice that Paul didn't gossip about John Mark, he didn't deride him, he simply, intentionally or not, handed him off to another leader.

I've had to fire my share of folks over the years. Typically, I would let them know that they wouldn't be working with me anymore, but they had a choice in how their ending would be framed. I almost always offered to help them find another job, another ministry, another leader to work with. Those situations where the person let us help them tended to go very well. We helped people find a better fit.

I listed these three options in reverse order of how we should approach them. If we are dealing with someone we may not really believe in, and we've done our best to remedy that without success, our first step may be trying to connect them with another leader. If that isn't a good option, we can try ignoring them. As a last step, we can remove them promptly.

7. Proceed Resolutely

If we participate in any type of leadership development, we will have set-backs, struggles, and downright failures. People will disappoint us. But we must keep at it.

> Forgetting the past and looking forward to what lies ahead, I press on to reach the end of the race and receive the heavenly prize for which God, through Christ Jesus, is calling us.
>
> —Philippians 3:13-14 (NLT)

In the iconic words of the legendary band, Journey, "Keep on believing."

THE KEY QUESTION:

Who is the primary customer for your ministry?

THE BIG CHALLENGE:

Communicate to some people in your network
that you truly believe in them.

CHAPTER TEN

FROM PROTECTION TO PARTNERSHIP

We can protect to survive or invest to thrive.

—Willie Nolte

We have to keep a close watch on each other, so that we don't degenerate into greedy parasites whose first care is to serve ourselves, rather than the masses of people who now depend on us.

—Cyrus the Great, *Xenophon's Cyrus the Great:
The Arts of Leadership and War*

It marks a big step in your development when you come to realize that other people can help you do a better job than you could do alone.

—Andrew Carnegie

wo guys who worked together were both laid off, so off they went to the unemployment office. When asked his occupation, the first guy said, "Underwear stitcher...I sew the elastic onto women's underwear." The clerk looked up *underwear stitcher*. Finding it classed as unskilled labor, she gave him $400 a week unemployment pay. The second guy was asked his occupation. "Diesel fitter," he replied. *Diesel fitter* was listed as a skilled job, so the clerk gave the second guy $680 a week. When the first guy found out he was furious. He stormed into the office to find out why his friend and co-worker was collecting nearly double his pay. The clerk explained, "Underwear stitchers are unskilled, and diesel fitters are skilled labor." "What skill?!" yelled the underwear stitcher. "I sew the elastic and he pulls on it and says, "Yep, dese'll fit 'er."

It wasn't about one preacher. There was in Antioch a teaching team.

It is so tempting to get caught up in jealousy, envy, and suspicion toward those we actually ought to be partnering with. We tend to underestimate the need for partners.

Adam Grant, in his book *Originals*, mentions, "the narcissism of small differences."[20] We can fall prey to believing that we have all the answers, so we mustn't need anyone else.

There's an old quip: "My mother was so overprotective we were only allowed to play rock, paper."

Some of us, in the name of protecting our stewardship, have become so overprotective we miss out on great partners.

Chris Gorman, Northwest Regional Minister for the North American Baptists, suggests, "Maybe the reason why there isn't more church planting is too many churches have refused to partner with other churches, and so they fail to spur one another on to love and good deeds."

Recently a church planter told me about a church in his city that requires church staff to sign a "non-compete" agreement, consenting to not work at another ministry in that area if they leave their church. Seriously? "Non-compete"

---

20   Adam Grant, *Originals: How Non-Conformists Move the World* (Penguin Books, 2017).

comes from the Dutch term from which we get, "nincompoop!" (Not really...actually maybe it does!)

John Jackson says that by the time we get to "Conflict of interest" statements it is already too late.

How about if we collaborate instead of combatting?

> "Do not stop him," Jesus said, "for whoever is not against you is for you."
>
> —Luke 9:50 (NIV)

The church in Antioch embraced partnering:

> Now in the church at Antioch there were prophets and teachers: Barnabas, Simeon called Niger, Lucius of Cyrene, Manaen (who had been brought up with Herod the tetrarch) and Saul.
>
> —Acts 13:1

If we are not careful, we may miss the implication from Acts 13: It wasn't about one preacher. There was in Antioch a *teaching team.*

Let's take a closer look at that team: *Barnabas* came on the scene in Acts chapter 4:

> All the believers were united in heart and mind. And they felt that what they owned was not their own, so they shared everything they had. The apostles testified powerfully to the resurrection of the Lord Jesus, and God's great blessing was upon them all. There were no needy people among them,

because those who owned land or houses would sell them and bring the money to the apostles to give to those in need.   For instance, there was Joseph, the one the apostles nicknamed Barnabas (which means "Son of Encouragement"). He was from the tribe of Levi and came from the island of Cyprus. He sold a field he owned and brought the money to the apostles.

—Acts 4:32-37 (NLT)

Barnabas was a Jewish Levite Christian from the Greek island of Cyprus. His given name was Joseph, but he was such an encourager, his nickname, which means "Son of Encouragement," stuck. He came on to the scene by giving generously – donating the entire proceeds from a land sale. He was the one who stood up for Saul to the Apostles (Acts 9) and pushed the Antioch church forward (Acts 11).

Simeon isn't so easy to pin down. Many scholars assume he is the Simon from Cyrene who helped Jesus carry his cross on the way to the crucifixion. Simon and Simeon are similar versions of the same name.

Others believe Simeon was a Jewish man with dark skin. He was called "Niger," which means "black, or the black one."

Still others believe Simeon was a black man since he was from Africa, albeit North Africa. Any way you look at it, Simeon looked a bit different from the others.

Then there is *Lucius.* He was from Cyrene, so he was from another continent. Amazingly, the name Lucius means "light, bright or white."

So there was the Greek guy, and the black guy, and the white guy…

And *Manaen,* who grew up with Herod the Tetrarch. There were a number of Herods in Biblical times. First there was Herod the Great. I always wanted the moniker, "The Great," but other than making my little sisters call me that for a time when we were growing up, it never took…

Herod the Great was named King of Judea by the Romans a few decades before Jesus was born.

He was clearly an insecure, paranoid, and evil ruler as evidenced by his "massacre of the innocents," as he had all the baby boys in his region killed near the time of Jesus' birth.

Herod died in 5 BC, and his kingdom was divided up between his sons. One of whom was Herod Antipas, also known as Herod the Tetrarch. Herod had married his brother's former wife, Herodias. She encouraged her daughter to ask for the head of John the Baptist on a platter, and Herod the Tetrarch caved in and ordered it.

They didn't have anything in common except for their commitment to Jesus and his kingdom.

Later, during the mock trial of Jesus, Herod questioned and mocked Jesus.

Manaen may have been a foster child of Herod the Tetrarch, or a close friend, or neighbor. But it is clear he saw a ton of dysfunctionality, and he grew up in an upper-class Jewish setting.

Speaking of Jewish settings, last on the list in Acts 13 is Saul.

Saul was a leader of the Pharisees. He was a model Jew.

This Saul later described himself this way:

> I am a pure-blooded citizen of Israel and a member
> of the tribe of Benjamin – a real Hebrew if there
> ever was one! I was a member of the Pharisees, who
> demand the strictest obedience to the Jewish law. I
> was so zealous that I harshly persecuted the church.
> And as for righteousness, I obeyed the law without
> fault.
>
> —Philippians 3:5-6 (NLT)

In Antioch, there was the Greek guy, the black guy, the white guy, the rich guy, and also the Jewish guy.

If there is one thing these men had in common, it is that they didn't have anything in common except for their commitment to Jesus and his kingdom. This variety describes the nature of the church at that time. There was a genuine love among the members that broke down walls of prejudice that could not have been broken any other way. Their leadership represented the diversity of their congregation.

The church that put Christianity on the map wasn't known for divisiveness, it was known for partnership.

Tod Bolsinger, in his excellent work, *Canoeing the Mountains*, compares modern day ministry with the Lewis and Clark expedition. As Lewis and Clark needed to radically change their leadership mentality as they faced new challenges, so does the church today:

Of all the landmark discoveries and mental-model reorientations that resulted from Lewis and Clark's discoveries, perhaps the most overlooked is their incredibly effective model of a leadership partnership. In the face of an American mythology of the lone leader who comes and singlehandedly saves the day, Lewis and Clark stand as an alternative mental model of partnership.[21]

Bolsinger referenced historian Stephen Ambrose:

What Lewis and Clark and the men of the Corps of Discovery had demonstrated is that there is nothing that people cannot do if they get themselves together and act as a team. Here you have thirty-two men who had become so close, so bonded, that when they heard a cough at night, they knew instantly who had a cold. They could see a man's shape in the dark and know who it was. They knew who liked salt on his meat and who didn't. They knew who was the best shot, the fastest runner, the one who could get a fire going the quickest on a rainy day. Around the campfire, they got to know about each other's parents and loved ones, and each other's hopes and dreams. They had come to love each other to the point where they would have sold their lives gladly to save a comrade. They had developed a bond, become a band of brothers, and

---

21   Tod Bolsinger, *Canoeing the Mountains: Christian Leadership in Uncharted Territory* (IVP Books, 2015)

together they were able to accomplish feats that astonish us today.[22]

King Solomon put it wisely:

It's better to have a partner than go it alone. Share the work, share the wealth.

And if one falls down, the other helps, but if there's no one to help, tough! Two in a bed warm each other. Alone, you shiver all night.
                                    —Ecclesiastes 4:9-11 (MSG)

Rita Coolidge admitted, "Too often, the opportunity knocks, but by the time you push back the chain, push back the bolt, unhook the two locks, and shut off the burglar alarm, it's too late."

Leadership coach Brian Burman says, "If your advice is more about protecting your position than equipping another leader to succeed, it is time to keep your mouth shut."

Too often we are more territorial than team-oriented.

Too often we are so mired in protection mode, we fail to see the enormous potential in embracing some strategic partnerships.

When the Holy Spirit spoke in Acts 13, there were no demands from the church leadership that any new works needed to be a certain distance away.

---

22   Ibid

R.A. Dickey, a pitcher on Toronto Blue Jays, was taken out after throwing only seventy-eight pitches. There were two outs in the fifth inning of game four of the 2015 baseball playoffs, when manager John Gibbons gave Dickey an early hook – and the Blue Jays had a six-run lead at the time. Dickey was within one out of qualifying to be the winning pitcher when he was replaced by David Price. After the game, reporters wondered how R.A. Dickey felt after being pulled. His response was classic:

> It is amazing what a team can accomplish if you do not care who gets the credit.
>
> —R.A. Dickey

Dickey was quoting Harry Truman:

> It is amazing what you can accomplish if you do not care who gets the credit.
>
> —Harry S Truman

Too often we are more territorial than team-oriented. We want credit. We've wanted recognition since the early days. Paul wrote:

> You are still worldly. For since there is jealousy and quarreling among you, are you not worldly? Are you not acting like mere humans? For when one says, "I follow Paul," and another, "I follow Apollos," are you not mere human beings? What, after all, is Apollos? And what is Paul? Only servants, through whom you

came to believe – as the Lord has assigned to each his task. I planted the seed, Apollos watered it, but God has been making it grow. So neither the one who plants nor the one who waters is anything, but only God, who makes things grow. The one who plants and the one who waters have one purpose, and they will each be rewarded according to their own labor. For we are co-workers in God's service...

—1 Corinthians 3:3-9 (NIV)

Tim Keller explained, "However, after WWI, especially among mainline Protestants, church planting plummeted, for a variety of reasons. One of the main reasons was the issue of 'turf'. Once the continental U.S. was covered by towns and settlements and churches and church buildings in each one, there was strong resistance from older churches to any new churches being planted in 'our neighborhood'"[23]

When we say, "You have to go at least so many miles away," it is essentially saying, "We do not want the gospel to be spread in our town."

Can we stop affirming turf wars? When we say, "You have to go at least so many miles away," it is essentially saying, "We do not want the gospel to be spread in our town." We have put up with such nonsense for far too long. We have allowed resistant pastors to stop church planting in their areas. Why? It didn't make sense to Paul; it shouldn't make sense to us.

---

23 Tim Keller, *Why We Plant Churches*

A three-year-old boy was as excited as he could be to visit his grandma in Florida, especially since it meant taking his first trip on an airplane. He had just boarded and got buckled in when he looked around the plane and cried. "What is it?" his mother asked, wondering if he was nervous. He asked with surprise, "If all these people are going to Grandma's house, will there be any cookies left for me?"

Our protective stances are really the things of three-year-old boys. Let's take some steps toward maturity.

The word "denomination" comes from the Latin, and it means "disappointment." No, I'm kidding. It is a compound Latin word, *de + nominare* simply meaning, "to name." We can keep our name, love our name, and even be proud of our heritage and tribe, and yet still partner with others.

I love Tom Robertson's transparent confession: "I needed to settle the glory issue. Either I got it or God got it. I was not meant to carry the glory belonging to God. It was so freeing to lay that burden down."

A couple years ago, we had another church move in next door – I mean *right* next door – to our church. It was the same church that moved right next door to us when we were meeting in a high school. Maybe their love language is physical touch and closeness? Anyway, our pastor, my son, Tim, made a decision. He went over, met the pastor, saw they were a little short of money, and said, "We need to give them some money, and it has to be a big gift." So our leadership team said, "Okay," and we wrote a large check to them.

Here is what I have learned from my son. It doesn't matter who gets the credit. (We initially named our network "Vandelay," primarily for the laugh, but also so we wouldn't take ourselves so stinking seriously.)

Napoleon Hill put it this way: "It is literally true that you can succeed best and quickest by helping others to succeed."

And John Pearson summed up Peter Drucker who said: "Autonomous, controlled organizations are the past. Networked people and organizations are the future. Independent organizations need to become interdependent. That requires trust, clear values, and objectives, and constant good communications among all involved in collaboration."

THE KEY QUESTION:

Who are my partners?

THE BIG CHALLENGE:

Give some money to a church or church planter
who is not of your immediate tribe.

CHAPTER ELEVEN

FROM GETTING TO GIVING

God loves you too much to let you win the lottery.

—Kenton Beshore, Mariners Church

My rule is, when in doubt, always give.

—C.S. Lewis

Success always calls for greater generosity - though most people, lost in the darkness of their own egos, treat it as an occasion for greater greed.

—Cyrus the Great, *Xenophon's Cyrus the Great:
The Arts of Leadership and War*

Two church planters are in a bank, when, suddenly, armed robbers burst in, waving guns and yelling for everyone to freeze. While several of the robbers take the money from the tellers, others line up the customers, including the church planters, against a wall, and proceed to take their wallets, watches, and other valuables. While this is going on, one of the church planters jams something into the other church planter's hand. Without looking down, the second church planter whispers, "What is this?" The first church planter replies, "It's the $100 I owe you."

Church Planters have to be good at getting. We are by nature, takers.

If you know how to get people, churches, and networks to give you money; if you can raise funds; if you know how to get music equipment donated; if you can fill a trailer with stuff others have given you for your new church, and if you were given the trailer for free; if you have the spiritual gift of receiving, then…you might be a church planter.

Sadly, too many of us church planters never transition from receiving to contributing. We get so good at asking, we get so comfortable with trying to get contributions, that we get stuck taking. We end up with a reputation of being spoiled, entitled grabbers who are only out for themselves. When established churches and leaders see our selfishness, they turn away from church planting and reproduction.

The older sister asks her younger brother, "What are you giving Mom and Dad for Christmas?" Without missing a beat, the little brother replies, "A list of everything I want."

Okay, money is tight – it is almost always tight – but in order to be successful in life we need to move from taking to giving.

Many church planters relate to comedian Tom Ryan who quipped, "I am heavily in debt. Right now my goal in life is to be broke. I want to get back to zero. Someday, I'm going to have nothing. I'll leave it to my kids. 'See this? None of this is all yours!'"

Jeff Sharp says, "I'm amazed at how fast church planters are willing to take money and how slow they are to invest it back into the other church planters."

Okay, money is tight – it is almost always tight – but in order to be successful in life we need to move from taking to giving.

Paul gave this admonition to the Ephesian church: "You should remember the words of the Lord Jesus: 'It is more blessed to give than to receive'" (Acts 20:35 NLT).

I believe the number one secret to raising funds for ministry is to be generous yourself. If I am a generous person, I will not be afraid to talk about money. If I am generous, I will be effective at saying, "Please" and "Thank you." If I am generous, I will be further down the road to making the whole fund-raising experience fun!

In the book *The Go-Giver*, we read:

> All the great fortunes in the world have been created by men and women who had a greater passion for what they were giving – their product, service or idea – than for what they were getting. And many of those great fortunes have been squandered by others who had a greater passion for what they were getting than what they were giving.[24]

And as Ray Johnston states:

Self-absorbed, happy people don't exist.[25]

24 Bob Burg and John David Mann, *The Go-Giver, Expanded Edition: A Little Story About a Powerful Business Idea* (Portfolio, 2015), Kindle Edition.

25 Ray Johnston, *Jesus Called – He Wants His Church Back: What Christians and the American Church Are Missing*, Kindle Edition (Thomas Nelson, 2016.

Rick Warren put it this way, "There are really only two kinds of people in life. There are givers and there are takers. You're going to be one or the other. You make the decision. The takers are the unhappy people in life. The givers are the happy people in life."

If you have the spiritual gift of receiving, then ... you might be a church planter.

Adam Grant wrote an informative book called *Give and Take* in which he describes three types of people: (1) *Givers*: those who tend to be inclined to give to others. (2) *Takers*: those who tend to try to get, to look out for themselves. And (3) *Matchers*: those who need to buy you lunch if you bought for them. They are "Even-Steven" people.

Surprisingly, Grant's studies showed that when it comes to success, those at the bottom of the ladder, the poorest performers, turned out to be the givers. So, guess what group was at the top? Takers? Matchers? No, it was givers again.

Then they privately tell me they feel that although they are not necessarily takers, they tend to feel stuck in the burnout stage.

How could that be?

In his book, Adam Grant explains why some givers are successful and others fail. Grant distinguishes between what he calls, "Selfless givers" – those who tend to give so much, without taking care of themselves, they burn out, and "Otherish givers" – successful, sustained givers.

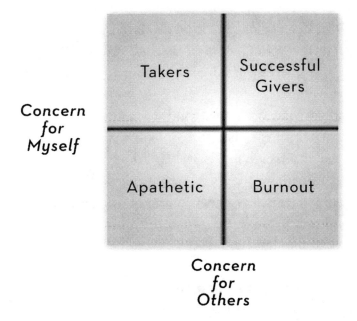

Concern
for
Myself

Takers

Successful
Givers

Apathetic

Burnout

Concern
for
Others

If we want to change the church planting world, we need to strive to be in the sustained, successful givers category.

Many of the church planters and ministry folks I have showed this diagram to readily admit that they do not see themselves as takers. Then they privately tell me they feel that although they are not necessarily takers, they tend to feel stuck in the burnout stage.

I love what Perry Noble quipped about burnout: "It's kind of like eating at Denny's. Nobody goes there intentionally, but you just kind of wind up there sometimes."

How to Avoid Burnout

So how can we move from burnout to becoming sustained, successful givers?

Let me make a few suggestions:

1. Practice regular spiritual disciplines.

Spend time with God, pray, fast, and read the Bible. It is impossible to last in ministry without regular connection times with God.

Take a day off – the day off made God's top ten list of commandments. Making a Sabbath a priority will ensure long-term strength for the task.

Eat right, sleep enough, exercise regularly – taking care of our bodies makes a huge impact of defeating burnout.

Give generously and consistently, both personally and through the churches we lead.

2. Get into a support network.

Grant observed, "Three decades of research show that receiving support from colleagues is a robust antidote to burnout. 'Having a support network of teachers is huge.'"[26]

We started Excel Leadership Network because of the huge need for church planters and leaders to be connected in a network that understands and supports them.

One of my favorite quotes from Grant's book comes from a sign he saw in a corporate office:

DOING A GOOD JOB HERE
Is Like Wetting Your Pants in a Dark Suit
YOU GET A WARM FEELING
BUT NO ONE ELSE NOTICES

Get in a group that notices!

---

26   Adam Grant, *Give and Take: Why Helping Others Drives Our Success* (Penguin Books, 2014).

3. Practice effective generosity.

Grant writes, "Givers don't burn out when they devote too much time and energy to giving. They burn out when they're working with people in need but are unable to help effectively."

Burnout comes when we give but it doesn't seem to be making a difference. As leaders, we need to show our donors what a huge difference their dollars and efforts are making.

4. Exercise exponential giving.

In his classic book, *The Legacy Journey*, financial guru Dave Ramsey encourages us to give thought to what we would or will do when more money flows our way:

> The goal is to look at the overflow and set ratios... You'll decide what percentage to give, what percentage to invest, and what percentage to use on lifestyle. The first thing you have to do, though, is decide what...you need to take care of your family...We're going to put ratios in place for anything over that amount, so be sure it isn't so high that there's no overflow and isn't so low that you and your family can't enjoy the blessings God's given you. You have to find the balance, which definitely means you need to talk to the Owner. Pray about it, and ask God to show you what income is appropriate for your family.[27]

As leaders, we need to show our donors what a huge difference their dollars and efforts are making.

---

27   Dave Ramsey, *The Legacy Journey: A Radical View of Biblical Wealth and Generosity* (Ramsey Press, 2014).

Have we ever even thought about what we will give if and when God blesses us more?

We can change the church planting world by giving so generously that others realize we are not out for ourselves, but for God.

Have you ever noticed that the best churches are often the most generous? Why are the top churches usually the most generous? Could it be that generous churches become the top churches?

One of the coolest things I've seen recently was Tury Nuñez, the pastor of a church in a poor area of Tijuana, bring an offering from his church and give that money away in Cuba. Tury tearfully told me, "Critics say we're in Tijuana and we're poor and we can't make a difference, but we just gave ten pastors half a month's salary each."

Did you know that Rivers Crossing Community Church in Mason, Ohio – one of the fastest growing churches in North America, led by Paul Taylor and Jeff Sharp – voted before they launched to give some money to a local church planter who wasn't even part of their network? They had $15,000 in the bank and voted to give away $5,000.

Karl Roth invested a ton of his own money to get Flipside Church in Madera, California, started. He admitted, "I made an 'executive' decision that the total offering we received from our first official offering would all be given to help Katrina families in the central valley. I wanted to set the trajectory of our church to be a giving church, not a receiving church… When the offering was counted, it was northward of $6,000. That's not a bad first offering for new church plant. We gave it all away. That one single act of giving set the tone for Flipside." Karl later challenged his people, "Wouldn't it be wonderful if we had to close the doors of our church because we were too giving?" Flipside is incredibly generous. Roth reports, "To date we are now giving away 42% of our general tithes and offerings to church plants and our mission work." Forty-two percent!

We are now requiring our church plants to start off by budgeting ten percent for giving.

Folks, we can change the church planting world with generosity.

Adam Grant concludes:

> It turns out that giving can be contagious. In one study, contagion experts James Fowler and Nicholas Christakis found that giving spreads rapidly and widely across social networks. When one person made the choice to contribute to a group at a personal cost over a series of rounds, other group members were more likely to contribute in future rounds, even when interacting with people who weren't present for the original act. "This influence persists for multiple periods and spreads up to three degrees of separation (from person to person to person to person)," Fowler and Christakis find, such that "each additional contribution a subject makes . . .in the first period is tripled over the course of the experiment by other subjects who are directly

or indirectly influenced to contribute more as a consequence."[28]

Our giving can begin to change the world!

Cyrus the Great noticed this: "There is a deep – and usually frustrated – desire in the heart of everyone to act with benevolence rather than selfishness, and one fine instance of generosity can inspire dozens more."[29]

Jim Kennon, Director of Development for Transformation Ministries observed, "I can't overstate the importance of establishing the value of generosity at the very beginning of planting a church. At its very heart, the gospel is about giving. *'For God so loved the world, he gave…'* It seems obvious, the church that is planted with giving in its heart is a church that will reflect the heart of the gospel."

THE KEY QUESTION:

Are you primarily a taker, a matcher, a giver on the road to burnout or a giver set up for sustained impact?

THE BIG CHALLENGE:

Give something significant away.

---

28   Adam Grant, *Give and Take: Why Helping Others Drives Our Success* (Penguin Books, 2014).

29   Xenophon, *Xenophon's Cyrus the Great: The Arts of Leadership and War*, ed. Larry Hedrick (St. Martin's Griffin, 2007).

CHAPTER TWELVE

FROM PROCEDURAL TO RELATIONAL

Jesus shifted religion from a system of belief and behavior to a system of relationships between humans and God, humans and humans, and humans and creation.

—Leonard Sweet

Everything rises and falls on leadership. And everything in leadership rises and falls on relationships.

—John Jackson

The primary way to prepare for the unknown is to attend to the quality of our relationships, to how well we know and trust one another. Trust is vital for change leadership. Without trust there is no "travel." When trust is lost, the journey is over.

—Margaret Wheatley

In his excellent book, *Outliers*, Malcolm Gladwell writes about a genius with an amazing IQ of 195. Christopher Langan could ace any foreign language test simply by skimming the textbook a couple minutes before the exam. He got a perfect score on his SAT, even though at one point he actually fell asleep taking it. Yet Langan didn't capitalize on his extraordinary talents and wound up working on a horse farm in rural Missouri.

According to Gladwell, Langan never enlisted a community of people to help him make the most of his intellectual prowess.

Gladwell summarizes Langan's story this way: "He had to make his way alone, and no one – not rock stars, not professional athletes, not software billionaires, and not even geniuses – ever makes it alone."[30]

We need more than intellectual competence to change the church planting world. We need other people.

Shawn Lovejoy believes:

> The number one mistake I see pastors make is living in isolation. We don't mean to, but we just get busy, overcommitted, overextended, exhausted, and sometimes even numb. After a long week of ministry, many of us just want to go home and binge on Netflix or self-medicate in some other way.... Jesus is our greatest example. Why did He pick the twelve apostles? Mark 3:14 tells us: *"And he appointed twelve (whom he also named apostles) so that they might be with him and he might send them out to preach..."*

We need more than intellectual competence to change the church planting world. We need other people.

Even Jesus knew He needed people with Him and for Him. What do pastors really need? If there

---

30   Malcolm Gladwell, *Outliers: The Story of Success* (Back Bay Books, 2011).

was one value I would list above all others it's this: friends. Not acquaintances, but really great friends who we respect and admire and who understand us. We need friends who are dealing with what we're dealing with and understand the pressure. We need friends who have walked where we will walk and have the scars to prove it, friends who will challenge us and hold us accountable. There is great pressure in the pastorate, but it doesn't have to break us.

And Ray Johnston warned, "The current, lone-ranger, church-avoiding, worship-neglecting, isolated, it's-all-about-me Christianity is not biblical faith. However vocal people may be about their theology, if they are not connected with other believers to worship, then they are not living authentic Christianity."[31]

The Excel Leadership Network focuses on spotting high-level leaders, setting them up for success, sending them out and supporting them in ministry. But why do we do it the way we do it? Why do we spend so much time together? Why do we intentionally go to sporting events together? Why do we require a several-day Discovery Center for any leader who wants to connect with us? Why do we have breakfasts and lunches and dinners together? Why do we push coaching and connecting? Why do we do what we do?

---

31 Ray Johnston, *Jesus Called – He Wants His Church Back: What Christians and the American Church Are Missing*, Kindle Edition (Thomas Nelson, 2016.

Secret Sauce

There's a secret ingredient, what Willie Nolte, Mission Lead for Transformation Ministries calls a "secret sauce" to what and why we do what we do in our church planting network and partnerships. When we publish our ten support systems and even our stated goals, we actually don't even list the secret ingredient. What is it?

The secret ingredient can be found in Acts chapter 9. Our network vision and philosophy comes from Acts 13 – setting apart leaders for their work. But Acts 13 is born out of Acts 8-9. There was a great persecution that prompted church planting. Acts 9 starts this way:

> Saul kept on threatening to kill the Lord's followers. He even went to the high priest and asked for letters to the Jewish leaders in Damascus. He did this because he wanted to arrest and take to Jerusalem any man or woman who had accepted the Lord's Way.
> —Acts 9:1-2 (CEV)

This is a story about someone who was at the very beginning of his spiritual journey. I think *resisting* is typically stage one in our spiritual lives, but Saul wasn't even to a resisting stage yet – he was at the *killing Christians* stage! But in the next verses he moved from killing believers to preaching boldly that Jesus is the Savior. What caused him to move? It's the same ingredient that explains why we do what we do.

When Saul had almost reached Damascus, a bright light from heaven suddenly flashed around him. He fell to the ground and heard a voice that said, "Saul! Saul! Why are you so cruel to me?" "Who are you?" Saul asked. "I am Jesus," the Lord answered. "I am the one you are so cruel to. Now get up and go into the city, where you will be told what to do." The men with Saul stood there speechless. They had heard the voice, but they had not seen anyone. Saul got up from the ground, and when he opened his eyes, he could not see a thing. Someone then led him by the hand to Damascus, and for three days he was blind and did not eat or drink.

—Acts 9:3-9 (CEV)

At first glance, it seems that the key catalyst to spiritual growth is a Damascus-road event, right? The thing that got Paul to the next level on his journey was this incredible blinding incident. That was the key, right? Sure, we try to provide environments that allow

This could end badly. "How about if I don't go talk to them, God?"

great experiences in our network, but that's not the secret I'm talking about. Saul's catalyst was more than the bright light event.

Maybe it was his encounter with the truth? Jesus hit Saul with the truth.

Truth is critical, but it wasn't the catalyst. Our network majors on truth. We teach the Bible. But the Bible says that even the demons know the truth. Our secret isn't about curriculum.

> A follower named Ananias lived in Damascus,
> and the Lord spoke to him in a vision. Ananias
> answered, "Lord, here I am."
>
> —Acts 9:10 (CEV)

There's talk of a vision, so was that it? Was some special dream the catalyst?

Visions are good, but not necessarily normative. Not everyone gets a special vision, so the catalyst is more than the vision piece.

> The Lord said to him (Ananias), "Get up and go
> to the house of Judas on Straight Street. When you
> get there, you will find a man named Saul from the
> city of Tarsus. Saul is praying, and he has seen a
> vision. He saw a man named Ananias coming to
> him and putting his hands on him, so that he could
> see again." Ananias replied, "Lord, a lot of people
> have told me about the terrible things this man has
> done to your followers in Jerusalem. Now the chief
> priests have given him the power to come here and
> arrest anyone who worships in your name."
>
> —Acts 9:11-14 (CEV)

Ananias pushes back, and who can blame him? He says, "Lord, that's a nice plan, but how about this: How about I not go and get myself jailed or killed! Can't I simply make a small donation or stop eating pork instead?"

Imagine that. Imagine there's someone who is out killing believers, and throwing every Christian he can find into jail. What would you say if God told you to go talk to him about Jesus?

Probably, "Thank you, no. I'm good."

I suspect that something similar has happened to a lot of us. Maybe we have felt that God wanted us to go talk to someone about Jesus, but we've thought, "Seriously? He's my boss. She's my neighbor. It's my best friend. This could end badly. "How about if I *don't* go talk to them, God?"

> The Lord said to Ananias, "Go! I have chosen him to tell foreigners, kings, and the people of Israel about me. I will show him how much he must suffer for worshiping in my name." Ananias left and went into the house where Saul was staying.
>
> —Acts 9:15-17 (CEV)

That took incredible courage. Ananias put his freedom and his life in God's hands.

> Ananias placed his hands on him and said, "Saul, the Lord Jesus has sent me. He is the same one who appeared to you along the road. He wants you to be able to see and to be filled with the Holy Spirit." Suddenly something like fish scales fell from Saul's eyes, and he could see. He got up and was baptized.
>
> —Acts 9:18 (CEV)

The miracle happened, then the conclusion:

Then he ate and felt much better. For several days
Saul stayed with the Lord's followers in Damascus.
Soon he went to the Jewish meeting places and
started telling people that Jesus is the Son of God.
Everyone who heard Saul was amazed and said,
"Isn't this the man who caused so much trouble for
those people in Jerusalem who worship in the name
of Jesus? Didn't he come here to arrest them and
take them to the chief priests?" Saul preached with
such power that he completely confused the Jewish
people in Damascus, as he tried to show them that
Jesus is the Messiah.

—Acts 9:19-22 (CEV)

This is the story of someone who took an incredible
leap on his spiritual journey. Saul went from arresting anyone who believed in Jesus to telling people that Jesus is the
Son of God. Saul did a reversal, a 180 degree, complete
turnaround for God.

What was the catalyst?

It wasn't just the experience.

It wasn't just the interaction with the truth.

It wasn't just the vision.

The change in Saul's life didn't occur when he was
blinded, when he had a vision, or even when he heard Jesus
talking.

Ananias placed his hands on him…

—Acts 9:17 (CEV)

Did you notice that the miracle in Saul's life didn't actually happen until Ananias showed up?

There was a relational component in Saul's spiritual journey turnaround.

The Secret Sauce for changing the church planting world is: *Relationships*.

We do the things the way we do them because *we are a relational network*. We focus on connecting because *we are a relational network*. We start out with several days of inten-sive encounters at the Discovery Center because *we are a relational network*. We go to ball games because *we are a relational network*. We push coaching because *we are a relational network*. We are unapologetically a relational network.

> **The Secret Sauce for changing the church planting world is: Relationships.**

Tod Bolsinger observed, "Leadership is always relational."

So, how do you program providential relationships?

You don't.

We can't schedule a miraculous meeting with Ananias every three to six months. Providential relationships are up to God. But we can work with God. We can put our-selves in a position to hear God through – and see God in – other people.

How?

How to Discover Godly Relationships
1. Sense the Ananias in my life

I originally had this as, "Look for the Ananias in our lives." But like Saul, we may need an Ananias because we're blind so we might not see him or her, but we can try to be aware and at least sense that God has somebody providentially picked out to help us.

> Anyone who walks with wise people grows wise.
> But a companion of foolish people suffers harm.
> —Proverbs 13:20 (NIV)

We need to get around wise, godly, effective leaders.

Steven Furtick says, "If you're going to do what God has called you to do, you have to intentionally bring the people into your life He wants you to have."

I suspect that God has an Ananias or two ready to make a difference in each of our lives. Are you sensing them? Are you available to them? Are you coming to clusters and hanging out with leaders?

2. Be an Ananias

I also suspect that you are called to be an Ananias is someone's life. Your touch, your words, just might cause the scales to drop from their eyes.

Brian Burman wrote, "If you are a task-oriented person who struggles with relationship, choose to prioritize relationships as your primary task."

A relational network can actually change our worlds.

Albert Schweitzer said, "In everyone's life, at some time, our inner fire goes out. It is then burst into flame by an encounter with another human being. We should all be thankful for those people who rekindle the inner spirit." Let's be that kindling.

THE KEY QUESTION:

What is the "secret sauce" in my ministry?

THE BIG CHALLENGE:

Play the Ananias role in someone's life as soon as possible.

CHAPTER THIRTEEN

FROM RAPID TO RESILIENT

God is not in a hurry. He is more interested in what you're becoming than where you're going. He will use the time of wandering and sitting to refine your character. He will use whatever time it takes to get you to where He needs you to be.

—Shane Philips

The absolute reality is that you're going to get the crap kicked out of you. It's never not happened.

—Steve Snider

It's easy to lose sight of the goal - or to lose heart in trying to reach it...When I was coaching, I met with the whole team before and after games every Wednesday I would remind our players of the big picture and help them set smaller goals within the larger mission. After a loss, I would often remind them that our short-term goals were still attainable and that we were still on track to reach our ultimate goal. When the team had been playing well, I would remind them not to fall in love with their own press clippings but to remember that both pride and complacency were enemies to our mission and would eventually lead to a fall. Whether we were winning or losing, we had to shake off the past and keep moving ahead.

—Tony Dungy

Just sit right back and you'll hear a tale, a tale of a fateful trip, that started from this tropic port, aboard this tiny ship. The mate was a mighty sailin' man, the Skipper brave and sure. Five passengers set sail that day for a three-hour tour. A three-hour tour. The weather started getting rough, the tiny ship was tossed. If not for the courage of the fearless crew, the Minnow would be lost. The Minnow would be lost. The ship set ground on the shore of this uncharted desert isle, with Gilligan, the Skipper too, the Millionaire and his wife, the movie star, the Professor and Mary Ann, here on Gilligan's Isle.

When I was growing up, *Gilligan's Island* was my favorite television show. It wasn't my favorite show because of the gripping plot – every episode was the same: They had a shot at getting off the island, but Gilligan would mess it up. It wasn't my favorite show because of the incredible acting, let's face it, these were not Oscar winners. And it wasn't my favorite show because of the deep lessons it presented. It was my favorite show because it came on at 3:30 – right when we got home from school – on KCOP, channel 13 in Los Angeles. The neighbor kids would come over, we'd all have a snack and watch Gilligan. Then my sisters would watch the Brady Bunch while I went outside with my friends to play baseball, football, or basketball, depending on the season.

Shipwrecks happen to everyone.

Gilligan's Island was a silly show – but it did make one clear point: Everybody has shipwrecks.

Shipwrecks happen to everyone.

It doesn't matter if you're the richest person around, you will have shipwrecks. It doesn't matter if you are married to the richest man around and you haven't done an ounce of work in your life, and they never see you sweat because you never have – you will have shipwrecks. It doesn't matter if you're the most beautiful woman around, a Hollywood celebrity – you will have shipwrecks. It doesn't matter if you're a hard-working farm girl from Kansas who pulled herself up by her own bootstraps, bootstraps break – you will have shipwrecks. It doesn't matter if you're the smartest person around and you can make a transistor radio out of coconut shells and a pint of sand – you will have shipwrecks. You might be a great leader, the captain of your ship – you will have shipwrecks. And it doesn't matter if you're an average, everyday Gilligan you will have shipwrecks

Did you think church planting was going to be easy?

Did you think church planting was going to be easy? Honestly, I have to admit that I kind of did. I was young, naïve, arrogant, and misguided. I may have subconsciously thought that since I'm really working for God, I am exempt from the shipwrecks.

Many of us go into the church planting field because we don't have the patience or endurance to wait for ministry success. We think it will be quick, safe, and easy. But we will have shipwrecks.

So the question is, how can we handle the shipwrecks in our lives?

Paul was busy turning the world upside down when he was persecuted for his faith. In Acts chapter 22, Paul was sentenced to flogging, whipping, or lashing, and an interesting dialogue occurs:

> When they tied Paul down to lash him, Paul said to the officer standing there, "Is it legal for you to whip a Roman citizen who hasn't even been tried?" When the officer heard this, he went to the commander and asked, "What are you doing? This man is a Roman citizen!" So the commander went over and asked Paul, "Tell me, are you a Roman citizen?" "Yes, I certainly am," Paul replied. "I am, too," the commander muttered, "and it cost me plenty!" Paul answered, "But I am a citizen by birth!"
>
> —Acts 22:25-28 (NLT)

So I guess there were immigration controversies back then too!

Long story short, Paul appeals to Caesar, and they ship him off to Rome. And he has a shipwreck.

Everybody has shipwrecks. Maybe you're in the midst of one, or trying to recover from one, or even entering into one – we all have shipwrecks. So how do we handle it?

> We had several days of slow sailing, and after great difficulty we finally neared Cnidus. But the wind was against us…We struggled along the coast with great difficulty and finally arrived at Fair Havens, near the town of Lasea. We had lost a lot of time. The weather was becoming dangerous for sea travel because it was so late in the fall, and Paul spoke to

the ship's officers about it. 'Men,' he said, 'I believe there is trouble ahead if we go on – shipwreck, loss of cargo, and danger to our lives as well.' But the officer in charge of the prisoners listened more to the ship's captain and the owner than to Paul."

—Acts 27:7-11 (NLT)

Let me pause to say that sometimes we don't deserve the shipwreck. Paul hadn't done anything wrong and he even warned the crew not to continue – he still ended up shipwrecked. Sometimes we're Gilligan and we cause it, but sometimes the shipwreck isn't our fault at all.

When a light wind began blowing from the south, the sailors thought they could make it. So they pulled up anchor and sailed close to the shore of Crete. But the weather changed abruptly, and a wind of typhoon strength (called a "northeaster") burst across the island and blew us out to sea... The next day, as gale-force winds continued to batter the ship, the crew began throwing the cargo overboard. The following day they even took some of the ship's gear and threw it overboard. The terrible storm raged for many days, blotting out the sun and the stars, until at last all hope was gone...No one had eaten for a long time. Finally, Paul called the crew together and said, "Men, you should have listened to me in the first place and not left Crete. You would have avoided all this damage and loss. But take courage! None of you will lose your lives,

even though the ship will go down. For last night
an angel of the God to whom I belong and whom I
serve stood beside me, and he said, 'Don't be afraid,
Paul, for you will surely stand trial before Caesar!
What's more, God in his goodness has granted
safety to everyone sailing with you.' So take courage! For I believe God. It will be just as he said. But
we will be shipwrecked on an island."
—Acts 27:13-14,18-26 (NLT)

Paul had a shipwreck, you have shipwrecks, I will have
them too. So how do we handle them?

Paul's advice to his crew, speaks to us today: *Keep up
your courage.*

But now I urge you to keep up your courage.
—Acts 27:22 (NIV)

Other versions have it as, "Cheer up!"(Acts 27:22
CEV) or "Don't give up!" (Acts 27:22 MSG).

John Wooden said, "Success is never final, failure is
never fatal. It's courage that counts."

And Henry Ward Beecher wrote, "We need not fear
shipwreck when God is the pilot."

So much of life is simply about resiliency. Paul's advice
to his fellow shipwrecksters was to not give up.

Once we were safe on shore, we learned that we
were on the island of Malta. The people of the
island were very kind to us. It was cold and rainy,

so they built a fire on the shore to welcome us. As Paul gathered an armful of sticks and was laying them on the fire, a poisonous snake, driven out by the heat, bit him on the hand. The people of the island saw it hanging from his hand and said to each other, "A murderer, no doubt! Though he escaped the sea, justice will not permit him to live."

—Acts 29:1-4 (NLT)

Sometimes bad gets worse. Here is Paul, arrested for preaching about Jesus, sent on a boat to Rome. The trip is a disaster, and there is a shipwreck. They have to swim to shore. It is freezing and it starts to rain. So, Paul builds a fire and a poisonous snake hops out of the fire and bites him.

Ever had seasons when things couldn't possibly get worse, but then they do?

Have you ever had experiences like that? When it hasn't been your day, your week, your month, or even your year? Ever had seasons when things couldn't possibly get worse, but then they do?

Look what Paul does:

But Paul shook off the snake into the fire and was unharmed. The people waited for him to swell up or suddenly drop dead. But when they had waited a long time and saw that he wasn't harmed, they changed their minds and decided he was a god.

—Acts 28:5-6 (NLT)

Paul simply shook it off. How do we handle shipwrecks?
Shake it off.
How do we handle snakebites?
Shake it off.
That proverbial, emotionless father or coach or boss whose only advice is "Shake it off!" has Biblical backing. "Walk it off, son."

When something or someone bites you, shake it off. When giving goes down, shake it off. When the doctor says there's a problem, shake it off. When the city and bank say "No go" on your church building project, shake it off. When your John Mark leaves your launch team, or Barnabas leaves your church, *shake it off!*

Now don't get me wrong, we have to mourn and grieve and work through what we need to work through. But we can't get stuck on our island, stuck in a pity party, stuck asking, "Why Me?" *Shake it off.*

How many people are paralyzed by the past? The Eagles sang, "Get over it!" And Paul says, "Shake it off!"

A van carrying a dozen movie stuntmen on the way to a film location in the mountains spun out of control on the icy road, crashed through a guard-rail, rolled down a 90-foot embankment, turned over, and burst into flames…

There were no injuries.

Is there something I just need to shake off?

This wasn't the only time Paul shook off defeat. In Acts 18 we read:

> Each Sabbath found Paul at the synagogue, trying
> to convince the Jews and Greeks alike. And after

Silas and Timothy came down from Macedonia, Paul spent all his time preaching the word. He testified to the Jews that Jesus was the Messiah. But when they opposed and insulted him, Paul shook the dust from his clothes and said, "Your blood is upon your own heads – I am innocent. From now on I will go preach to the Gentiles.

—Acts 18:4-6 (NLT)

Ministry letdowns are tough to take. Too often we feel like a total failure. The Apostle Paul must have been tempted to feel that way. He spent "all his time" preaching. But there was no response – actually, there was no positive response.

So he quit, right? He moved south to become a pool man, he gave up ministry altogether, he stayed mired in his disappointment, didn't he?

No, Paul simply shook it off.

One of the hidden keys to effective church planting is simple resiliency. We go into church planting because we want to see instant results, but we need to hang in there for real results.

Two church members were going door to door, and knocked on the door of a woman who was not happy to see them. She told them, in no uncertain terms, that she did not want to hear their message and slammed the door in their faces. To her surprise, however, the door did not close and, in fact, bounced back open. She tried again, really put her back into it, and slammed the door again with the same

Ministry letdowns are tough to take. Too often we feel like a total failure.

result – the door bounced back open. Convinced these rude young people were sticking their foot in the door, she reared back to give it a slam that would teach them a lesson, when one of them said, "Ma'am, before you do that again, you need to move your cat."

Here is a key to changing the church planting world: Hang in there, exercise resilience, shake it off.

THE KEY QUESTION:

Do I expect it to be easy?

THE BIG CHALLENGE:

Shake off the next shipwreck or snakebite you experience.

CHAPTER FOURTEEN

FROM ONE-SIZE-FITS-ALL TO BEST FIT

Everyone is a 10 - somewhere.

—Wayne Cordeiro

The real test of a man is not when he plays the role he wants for himself, but when he plays the role destiny has for him.

—Vaclav Havel

God is in the business of strategically positioning us in the right place at the right time, but it's up to us to see and seize those opportunities that are all around us all the time."

—Mark Batterson

S teven Spielberg admitted about his childhood, "I was the last one picked for football, the last one picked for baseball, the last one picked for badminton." But his mother saw some talent in him, "Steven always had a highly developed imagination," she said. Then someone gave Steven a movie camera and his mother said, "He had a ball" with his family and friends.

Alan Loy McGinnis writes about successful people: "Rather than becoming obsessed with their weaknesses, they compensate by developing their strengths. They keep experimenting until they find something where they have aptitude, then make that proficiency the foundation for further achievements. The psychological law here is that the more we dwell on our weaknesses, the weaker we become; and the more we develop our strengths, the more personal power we find."

When it comes to making an impact, entrepreneurial leaders are necessary. The Bible talks about Paul and Silas sticking their necks out, starting things when nothing was happening, and living on the edge.

Acts 17 describes them as men who turned the world upside down:

> Paul and Silas then traveled through the towns of Amphipolis and Apollonia and came to Thessalonica, where there was a Jewish synagogue. As was Paul's custom, he went to the synagogue service, and for three Sabbaths in a row he used the Scriptures to reason with the people. He explained the prophecies and proved that the Messiah must suffer and rise from the dead. He said, "This Jesus I'm telling you about is the Messiah." Some of the Jews who listened were persuaded and joined Paul and Silas, along with many God-fearing Greek men and quite a few prominent women. But some of the Jews were jealous, so they gathered some troublemakers from the marketplace to form a mob and start a riot. They attacked the home of Jason, searching for Paul and Silas so they could drag them out to the crowd. Not finding them

But they didn't do it alone. And they didn't expect everyone to be exactly like them.

there, they dragged out Jason and some of the other believers instead and took them before the city council. "Paul and Silas have caused trouble all over the world," they shouted, "and now they are here disturbing our city, too. And Jason has welcomed them into his home. They are all guilty of treason against Caesar, for they profess allegiance to another king, named Jesus." The people of the city, as well as the city council, were thrown into turmoil by these reports. So the officials forced Jason and the other believers to post bond, and then they released them.

—Acts 17: 1-9 (NLT)

This New Living Bible says that Paul and Silas caused trouble for Jesus.

Paul and Silas were the church planters of the first century. They came into town, set up shop, started a church, and did it all over again somewhere else. They made a difference for Jesus, and they made an impact for the kingdom.

But they didn't do it alone. And they didn't expect everyone to be exactly like them.

Oswald Chambers suggested, "Let God be as original with other people as He is with you."

The Right Position

There were other kinds of leaders that led to this kingdom movement: There were the *Jasons*.

This is the only time Jason is mentioned in the Bible. We don't know very much about Jason, but this passage does give us some insights.

Jason was a leader.

Twice in this story we read about, *"Jason and the other believers..."* The fact that he was the one who was named and his name came first ensures that Jason was a leader. He was obviously vocal about his faith. An angry mob went looking to "drag Paul and Silas out to the mob, and so they went straight to Jason's home" (Acts 17:5 CEV).

He wasn't Paul. He wasn't Paul's right hand man. But he helped turn the world upside down...

When they were looking for the Christian leaders, they went to Jason's house first – he was clearly a leader who put his reputation on the line for Jesus.

Jason opened up his home.

Jason was that "man of peace" that Jesus talked about when he sent out the seventy-two:

> When you enter a house, first say, "Peace to this house." If a man of peace is there, your peace will rest on him; if not, it will return to you. Stay in that house, eating and drinking whatever they give you, for the worker deserves his wages. Do not move around from house to house.
>
> —Luke 10:5-7 (NIV)

Jason was hospitable. He let Paul and Silas stay with him. Evidently his house was where that first Thessalonian church met.

Jason opened up his wallet.

> They made Jason and his friends post heavy bail
> and let them go while they investigated the charges.
> —Acts 17:9 (MSG)

This passage tells us that Jason forked over money for his faith. Perhaps he wasn't happy about it, maybe he got it back (there is no indication that the money was ever returned from the government). But he did spend money for ministry.

Jason stayed in town.

> That night, under cover of darkness, their friends
> got Paul and Silas out of town as fast as they could.
> They sent them to Berea, where they again met with
> the Jewish community. They were treated a lot bet-
> ter there than in Thessalonica.
> —Acts 17:10-11 (MSG)

Paul and Silas and Barnabas and Mark traveled all over, but Jason stayed in town. Paul and Silas got things started. Jason and the other believers took it from there. Paul and Silas made things happen. Jason cleaned up the mess and kept things going.

Paul and Silas turned the world upside down. But so did Jason. Perhaps he was not a gifted evangelist. Maybe preaching wasn't his thing. He was probably not a catalytic church planter. He wasn't Paul. He wasn't Paul's right hand

man. But he helped turn the world upside down by leading, opening his home (his facilities), opening his wallet,
and maintaining the momentum.

We have to be on the lookout for the Pauls and Silases
and Barnabases and Marks of this day. But we're also looking for some Jasons.

How will churches get started and people get reached
without someone to be a leader like Jason? How can a
work get going without some men and women of peace?
What are churches to do unless someone opens their home
or their business or their office or their school or their facilities for churches? How far will the kingdom get without a
great number of people opening their wallets for the cause?
And how can a movement happen if some aren't willing to
stay?

In the three churches my wife Lori and I planted, we've
seen all kinds of Jasons open their homes for everything –
from church services to baptisms to youth groups to every
type of meeting before, during, and after we secured church
facilities. Recently I was at a YMCA meeting where the
branch director is opening the facilities to one of our new
churches because he's a Jason. We've encountered many
Jasons who have generously opened wallets and purses
and bank accounts (usually without force!) to make things
happen for all kinds of church planting and mission work.
While a lot of us planters are out catalyzing, entrepreneur-
ing, and causing trouble, so many faithful Jasons are holding down the fort. I wonder how many times some official
wanted to drag me away by my ears, but some Jason took
the hit for me – probably a good number of occasions.

God wants to use you and me to cause some trouble for Jesus, to turn our world upside down, to make a significant difference. That means we all need to discover our part and play it. If you're a Paul or a Silas, great! But if you're a Jason, that is just as great! The kingdom wouldn't be the same without you.

So all of you Jasons, thanks for all you do. Take a bow! And take a step forward too, we really need you.

The Right Model

The new found "Missional Community" or "House Church" approach to church planting reminds me of bathroom hand dryers. Honestly! When I see an automatic hand-dryer in a public bathroom, a few thoughts enter my mind.

First, I know we need to come up with a better way. High-cost, high-maintenance paper towels probably aren't great for the environment long-term, and they are likely resource-wasters, so I applaud the attempts to find a new solution to drying hands.

Second, we seem to be making some progress in the hand-dryer solution. The dryers have gotten progressively better over the last few years.

But ultimately, I am still – and you probably are too – wiping my hands on my pants.

Hand-dryers just take too long, or at least they seem to take five-times as long as the old way.

When all is said and done it seems all we get is a bunch of hot air.

Not to mention they scare the children!

And when I encounter an automatic hand dryer in an establishment, I often wonder if the owners are using this new-fangled approach for their benefit or the benefit of their customers?

I'd encourage the bathroom research and development people to keep at it, but with the hand dryers, please leave a few paper towels on the counter – the old way is still effective.

Similarly, I realize that we have to come up with a new way of doing ministry in North America in the twenty-first century. Attractional ministries can be high-cost, high-maintenance, and maybe they waste more resources than they should.

> **We have to come up with a new way of doing ministry in North America in the twenty-first century.**

And I admit that we've seen some progress in the *MC* (missional community) world. There are a few folks who are making this work. We are certainly doing better than we were ten or twenty years ago with this new approach.

But the old way of primarily attractional stuff seems to still be the most effective thing we are doing.

The missional community idea is way slower, and often all we get is a bunch of hot air.

I think it might be scaring the kids, too!

And let's ask if we are trying this new approach simply to make ourselves look cool, or because it is best for those we are trying to reach?

My bottom line is this: I don't think we've got the next effective strategy for ministry figured out yet. The MC and house church thing is getting closer, but it isn't all that effectual as of yet.

I love this quip: "In a bathroom I saw a sign that said employees must wash hands, but after I waited...no one came to wash my hands so I did it myself."

We need a new approach, and we need to keep at the research and development to identify it! In the meantime, let's not completely throw out the old strategies that have worked and still do to some extent today. Leaving a few paper towels on the counter makes great sense!

Recently I tried an automatic hand dryer in a Canadian restaurant – it worked really well. I looked for the brand name on the machine – it made me smile: "Excel!"

The Right Place

A man has to attend a large convention in Chicago. On this particular trip he decides to bring his wife. When they arrive at their hotel and are shown to their room, the man says, "You rest here while I register. I'll be back within an hour." The wife lies down on the bed. Just then, an elevated train passes by very close to the window and shakes the room so hard she's thrown out of the bed. Thinking this must be a freak occurrence, she lies down once more. Again a train shakes the room so violently, she's pitched to the floor. Exasperated, she calls the front desk and asks for the manager. The manager says he'll be right up. The manager, naturally, is skeptical, but the wife insists the story is true. "Look, lie here on the bed. You'll be thrown right to the floor!" the woman says. So he lies down next to the wife. Just then the husband walks in. "What are you doing here?" the husband asks. The manager replies, "Would you believe I'm waiting for a train?"

Have you ever been in the *wrong* place?

Many gifted church planters have the right position and the right model, but they are not in the right place.

I suspect that if we planted our second church twenty miles northeast in a different suburb, it would have been even more effective.

So how can we discover the best place for a plant?

Many organizations use exhaustive demographic research to determine a place. But demographics can be a bit deceiving. When we moved to the Bay Area we chose the fastest growing county, and a city that had been voted the number one place to live in the San Francisco region. We moved in on a Saturday, and the following Tuesday that city voted to adopt a no-growth city plan. The entire time we lived there all of the politicians fell into two categories: no growth forever, or no growth for the next ten years.

Other organizations simply rely on the "call" or the "heart" of the church planter to decide a place. Most of the church planters we deal with – eighty to ninety percent – come to us with an already-identified place in mind. But church planters can be wrong. When I drove by the pristine little league baseball fields of the town we were considering for our second church plant, I was sold. I heard the call! It may have been an umpire's "Safe!" call rather than God. My heart said yes. I didn't bother too much with my head after that.

> **Many gifted church planters have the right position and the right model, but they are not in the right place.**

Is there a better way to determine where to plant?

My colleague Jay Nickless has come up with a Target Analysis Plan (TAP Team Process) that has proven to be very helpful.

> So Barnabas and Saul were sent out by the Holy Spirit. They went down to the seaport of Seleucia and then sailed for the island of Cyprus.
>
> —Acts 13:4 (NLT)

Nickless writes, "While the churches' process of sending Barnabas and Saul was what we might call very "spiritual" in its essence, their decision to go to Cyprus had what we might call some very "logical" reasons as well.

We would do well to become more intentional about where churches are planted.

- Cyprus was Barnabas' home (Acts 4:36)

- Cyprus was close to Antioch (2 days journey)

- Cyprus had a large Jewish population (seeds of the gospel)

When it comes to knowing where to plant a church, I have come to believe that there are both spiritual and logical reasons…and the two are not necessarily mutually exclusive."

The TAP process includes four phases: Consideration, Research, Exploration, and Confirmation.

The point is we would do well to become more intentional about where churches are planted.

The wrong person in the wrong place = regression

The wrong person in the right place = frustration

The right person in the wrong place = confusion

The right person in the right place = progression

The right people in the right places = multiplication

Here is the point, instead of trying to jam every willing participant into our molds, our schemes, our stratagems, our models, and even our target areas, let's serve those leaders and help them to find their best fit.

THE KEY QUESTION:

Do you consistently put the right people
in the right places at the right time?

THE BIG CHALLENGE:

Purposely hang out with a leader who
is very different from you.

CHAPTER FIFTEEN

FROM ASSESSMENT TO DISCOVERY

Not that smart. Not that hot. Not that nice. Not that funny. That's me: I'm not that.

—John Green

Our problem is not that we aren't where we should be, but that we aren't what we should be where we are."

—Os Guinness, *The Call: Finding and Fulfilling the Central Purpose of Your Life*

You can't improve what you won't face and own.

—Michael Hyatt, *Living Forward: A Proven Plan to Stop Drifting and Get the Life You Want*

I may have personally assessed more church planting couples in the last twenty-five years than anyone else in the United States. Maybe my counselor friend, Jerry Dahl from Strategic Team Makers has me beat. Maybe there is someone out there I don't know about, but I've personally been on the staff of or leading assessment centers for more couples than just about anyone. For years, I led assessment centers, first for a major Christian denomination, then we brought the system to the Green Lake Conference Center and we were able to serve over thirty different denominational groups. Then we branched out on our own.

I have seen thousands of couples go through a three- to four-day process where we've employed multiple days, multiple exercises, multiple interviews, and multiple advisors to come out with multiple recommendations on whether or not the candidate or couple should start a church.

It is time for a change. No, I'm not coming out against the process. I believe in the multiple days and advisors process so much that I've been part of a ton of them. What I think we need to change is the name, and the approach. So we did.

In our network we no longer use the "ass…" word. We have done away with "assessment." And we've moved to "discovery." Or maybe, "discernment" might be a more accurate word.

I have encountered a good number of struggling, church planting candidates at assessments over the years.

I am not an expert on you. No one is an expert on you, except you and God.

I've seen people with wild backgrounds, affiliations with the mafia; pastors who have run off with their secretary only to show up at an assessment now married to that secretary; some who don't appear to understand the gospel; some who are married to someone who isn't a believer yet; many who couldn't explain the gospel, let alone grasp it – I've seen some craziness in candidates.

Crazy candidates are fairly easy to deal with. We run them through the system and help them out. But crazy staff members at assessments present an entirely different story. There are few things more disruptive to a church planter assessment process than a so-called "assessor" who is dealing with his or her stuff right out in front of God and everybody. When assessors act like asses one can assume the assembly needs an assist.

Some staffers show up to their first assessment and proceed to tell experienced staffers how it should be done... within the first ten minutes. Some have taken other staffers aside and offered to bribe them into giving "their candidate" a better result. Some simply cry uncontrollably. One refused to tell his candidate when we came up with a "Not Recommended" outcome for them. I guess he just wanted to tell them, "Never mind."

Some people, upon receiving the label of "assessor," immediately transform into Ron Burgandy, Will Ferrel's character from the movie, *Anchorman*. "Do you know who I am? ...I'm kind of a big deal, people know me..."

The very term "assessor" denotes superiority. It implies that we are here to tell you what you should do. It encourages arrogance and condescension.

Think about it. I am not an expert on you. No one is an expert on you, except you and God. Setting myself up to pretend to be able to tell you what to do and how to do it is something between silly and delusional.

Can we kill this assessment haughtiness that is so prevalent in our systems?

"Mommy, my turtle's dead," the little boy sorrowfully told his mother, holding the turtle out to her in his hand. The mother kissed him on the head and said, "That's all right. We'll wrap him in tissue paper, put him in a little box, and have a nice burial ceremony in the back yard. After that, we'll go out for an ice cream soda, and then get you a new pet." "Ice cream?" the little boy said, wiping his tears and smiling. "Oh boy!" His mother said: "I don't want you…" Her voice trailed off as she noticed the turtle move. "Honey, your turtle isn't dead after all!" "Oh," the disappointed boy said. "Can I kill it?"

> **Our job as servants is to help candidates discover their next step of ministry, rather than pontificate about our own brilliance.**

Can we kill this assessment haughtiness that is so prevalent in our systems?

It was the Holy Spirit who spoke in Acts chapter 13, not assessors. The prophets and teachers in the Antioch church were not mandating what the other leaders ought to do. They were bent on hearing from God and encouraging others to follow that direction. A couple chapters later, the church leaders concluded this way: "For it seemed good to the Holy Spirit and to us…" (Acts 15:28 NLT).

It seems to me that our job as servants is to help candidates discover their next step of ministry, rather than pontificate about our own brilliance.

We've changed labels – from "Assessment Center" to "Discovery Center," and from "Assessor" to "Staff." First-timers are simply "Observers." And we've assembled a "dream team" of experienced staff who are learning to check their personal issues at the door as they embrace a servant's attitude.

It is a subtle change, but it makes a huge difference. Candidates are no longer immediately put on the defensive because they have to undergo an assessment. They can relax and allow others to supportively help them discover their next best steps.

There's an old witticism: "I may not be that funny or athletic or good looking or smart or talented …. I forgot where I was going with this."

Yes, we need to help people become more self-aware, but we can do it in an encouraging and supportive manner.

Another issue with "assessments" is they denote a stand-alone, "one-and-done" event. Assessment centers, by themselves, are of some value. But they definitely need the other systems or environments. Sending a candidate to an assessment center without having the other support structures in place can backfire. A couple will go through this well-executed appraisal process, and then expect the sending agency to have follow-up procedures like coaching and gatherings in place. When those are lacking, the couple can feel like there has been a bait and switch.

Assessments are designed to work alongside other systems. They set up all the other systems. That's why the term, "discovery" is more appropriate. The Discovery Center helps the sending group with a six-month (at least) head start on coaching; it shows leaders what areas of support are particularly critical for each couple; it gives everyone direction on the types of training necessary for each candidate; and it provides discernment on what kinds of partnerships would make sense for each planter.

Will Mancini says, "Discovery and exploration do not so much answer all of our questions as they help us to raise and consider new questions."

We don't have to pretend to have all of the answers, but we can serve each candidate, by helping them find their best fit.

THE KEY QUESTION:

When was the last time I started acting like
I was kind of a big deal...?

THE BIG CHALLENGE:

Stop using the "Ass..." words.

CHAPTER SIXTEEN

FROM RECLUSIVE TO REPRODUCING

Institutions age and die just like people. New babies (churches) are good for everybody. It's the natural (and supernatural) thing to do - reproduce.

—Leith Anderson

Plant pregnant! Don't just plant one church, plant a church that plants churches.

—Paul Taylor, Rivers Crossing Community Church

A church is not mature until it has had a baby.

—Rick Warren

Three University of Southern California fans are at the doctor for some tests. The doctor asks the first USC fan, "What is three times three?" "274," was his reply. The doctor says to the second man, "It's your turn. What is three times three?" "Tuesday," replies the second man. The doctor says to the third USC supporter, "Okay, your turn. What's three times three?" "Nine," says the third man. "That's great!" says the doctor. "How did you get that answer?" "Simple," says the third USC fan, "I subtracted 274 from Tuesday."

Multiplication can be tricky, but it is our calling.

One of the first things God said to human beings was, "Now be fruitful and multiply…" (Genesis 9:7 NLT).

We were made to multiply.

Woody Allen admitted, "Some guy hit my fender, and I told him, 'Be fruitful and multiply,' but not in those exact words."

Multiplication is our calling; it is part of who we are.

In the parable of the talents Jesus spoke of the importance of multiplication:

> After a long time the master of those servants returned and settled accounts with them. The man who had received the five talents brought the other five. "Master," he said, "you entrusted me with five talents. See, I have gained five more." His master replied, "Well done, good and faithful servant! You have been faithful with a few things; I will put you in charge of many things. Come and share your master's happiness!"
>
> —Matthew 25:19-23

Multiplication is our calling; it is part of who we are.

Notice that the "Well done!" comes after multiplication. We see it in Jesus' parable of the sower:

> Still other seed fell on good soil. It came up, grew and produced a crop, multiplying thirty, sixty, or even a hundred times.
>
> —Mark 4:8

Notice that the goal is reproduction, the goal is multiplication.

We hear it in the Great Commission as well:

> As you sent me into the world, I have sent them into the world.
>
> —John 17:18

> Perhaps the ultimate test is not what you are able to do in the here and now – but instead what continues to grow long after you've gone.[32]
>
> —Tom Rath and Barry Conchie

If we're not multiplying, we're not doing it right. If we are not reproducing our lives, our groups, our churches, and even our movement, then we're not following Jesus' orders.

We were made to multiply. But most church groups do not understand this.

> My Father is glorified by this, that you bear much fruit, and so prove to be my disciples.
>
> —John 15:8 (NASV)

> Jesus expected his followers to reproduce.[33]
>
> —Robert E. Coleman

Jesus expected reproduction. We either reproduce or we're thrown into the fire and burned. Reproduction is the proof that we really are followers.

---

32   Tom Rath and Barry Conchie, *Strengths Based Leadership: Great Leaders, Teams, and Why People Follow* (Gallup Press, 2008).

33   Robert E. Coleman, *The Master Plan of Evangelism* (Revell, 2010).

There's an old proverb that says, "If you want something done right, do it yourself." Many folks live by that. But it isn't a Biblical concept:

> I tell you the truth, anyone who has faith in me will
> do what I have been doing. He will do even greater
> things than these, because I am going to the Father.
>   —John 14:12

Jesus lived with the philosophy that if you want something done you need to multiply yourself by pouring your life into others.

Many churches act like a recluse. They hunker down in their own compound-like facilities, refusing to interact with anyone on the outside.

Perhaps they misunderstand what it really means to parent a church, like the lady who said, "I think the scariest thing about having triplets is being pregnant for twenty-seven months."

Jesus lived with the philosophy that if you want something done you need to multiply yourself by pouring your life into others.

Dave Ferguson, Todd Wilson, and others came up with the latest statistics on multiplying churches. They noted five categories of churches in North America: (1) *Declining*, (2) *Plateauing*, (3) *Adding*, or growing by addition, (4) *Reproducing* with sites or plants, and (5) *Movement-maker churches* – a church that planted to the fourth generation.

The statistics showed that a full eighty percent of churches were either plateauing or declining. Sixteen percent were adding, growing some. Four percent were reproducing, but only half of these reproduced on purpose. If you are good at math, you realize that leaves zero percent in category 5.

Along with this study, Ferguson and Wilson tried to identify the top reproducing churches in the United States:

> As we pressed into our Exponential 2015 theme of igniting a culture of multiplication, our team set out to identify ten radically multiplying U.S. churches – just 10 that we could highlight and learn from. With more than 350,000 churches in the United States, that ten represents just .003 percent of churches. We spent months searching for them, but we couldn't find ten. We couldn't find even three. Something's not right. This isn't how it's meant to be.[34]

One of our issues is that the things that help us grow are often the very things that keep us from getting to category 4. We want to get famous, to be on the top-growing list, to get the speaking engagements and the book deals.

Leith Anderson admitted, "Pastors of large churches tend to define themselves by church attendance (which makes church planting unattractive if they let people go). I chose to find greater satisfaction in starting new churches. At the end of a career it is more satisfying to have started numerous churches with tens of thousands of people who

---

34 Todd Wilson and Dave Ferguson, *Becoming a Level Five Multiplying Church: Field Guide*, Kindle Edition (Exponential Resources, 2015.

don't know me rather than have a few thousand more people who do know me."

Here's the point. We can make a difference. We can move the ball downfield. We can take new ground. We can influence networks and denominations and associations of churches. We can change the church planting world.

Zechariah 4:10 asks, "Does anyone dare despise this day of small beginnings?"

THE KEY QUESTION:

Where is my church on the five category scale?

THE BIG CHALLENGE:

Have at least one Coke, coffee, or conversation with at least one potential church planter at least once per month.

PART THREE:

SO WHAT? NOW WHAT?

The best plan is only good intentions unless it degenerates into work.

Peter Drucker

I arise in the morning torn between a desire to improve the world and a desire to enjoy the world, this makes it difficult to plan the day.

E.B. White

For every complex problem there is an answer that is clear, simple, and wrong.

H. L. Mencken

CHAPTER 17

GETTING UNSTUCK

There are really only two types of people - those who accept the need to change, and those who don't. The former grow, the latter stay trapped in a prison of stagnation.

—Archibald Hart

The road to success is dotted with many tempting parking places.

—Bendixline

If I wanted to make a difference...wishing for things to change wouldn't make them change. Hoping for improvements wouldn't bring them. Dreaming wouldn't provide all the answers I needed. Vision wouldn't be enough to bring transformation to me or others. Only by managing my thinking and shifting my thoughts from desire to deeds would I be able to bring about positive change. I needed to go from wanting to doing.

—John C. Maxwell, *Intentional Living: Choosing a Life That Matters*

A few years ago I went to a 49ers Monday Night Football game when the team was still playing at Candlestick Park in San Francisco. The traffic was so bad coming out of the game that it took over an hour to get from the parking lot to the nearby 101 freeway. The next year I went to another Monday Night Football game at Candlestick. This time I had a plan for getting out quickly. I strategically parked further away from the stadium. I picked a parking spot where no one would park in front of me or behind me. And I left the game at the end of the third quarter to ensure my quick getaway. Yes, I admit it – I cared way more about a smooth exit than I did the score of the game. Anyway, I snuck out of the game, and rushed to my car only to see that someone had parked illegally in front of me, and someone else had parked even more illegally behind me. I was blocked in! I got in the car and screamed – you may have heard me.

Within minutes, the people who had parked beside me returned to their car and left. So, I examined this situation and noticed that I could actually get out if I was able to turn my car around. So I maneuvered a lengthy twenty-seven point turn and escaped! I was so pleased with myself, I was free – for about thirty yards when I came to a dead stop. Everyone who was attempting the early exit had stopped. I waited, then got out of the car to see what the holdup was. The word came back to our place in line that some person or persons had actually parked in a way to block the only exit from this parking lot. There was no way out! We were stuck. There was nothing any of us could do. So, I got back in the car and turned on the radio to listen to the game. Of course the game went into

The church planting world seems to be stuck in patterns that have not served us, God, or the world very well.

overtime. I was stuck in the exact spot – unable to move – for the next two hours. I got my iPad out and actually got some work done, but I don't think I got home until Thursday afternoon.

I thought my situation was bad until I heard about that traffic jam in China a few years ago that lasted for sixty miles and it took more than a week for people to get unstuck. The combination of construction projects, a spike in the number of trucks using the road, minor traffic accidents, and broken-down vehicles left thousands wedged in. Drivers resorted to playing cards and chess, and some opportunistic entrepreneurs showed up on bikes with food and drinks and just gouged the daylights out of folks charging a mint for instant noodles and water. Motorists joked that they should have set up some stages and held concerts while they were waiting.

The church planting world seems to be stuck in patterns that have not served us, God, or the world very well.

The question is: How do we get unstuck?

In his book, *Change or Die*, Alan Deutschman reveals that when confronted with that choice – to change or die – ninety percent of people choose to die. Stop smoking, stop drinking, put the Baconator or Three Way cheeseburger down or die, ninety percent refuse to change. He says people don't change out of fear, facts, or force.[35]

He concludes there are three keys to change: Relate, Repeat, Reframe: new hope, new skills, new thinking.

---

35   Alan Deutschman, *Change or Die: The Three Keys to Change at Work and in Life* (HarperBusiness, 2007).

Relate

Real change comes through relationships.

The good news is there are leaders out there who want to change the church planting world, and they want to connect with you.

In his book, *Lasting Impact*, Carey Nieuwhof emphasizes the need for new relationships: "Familiarity breeds contempt and distorts perspective. If your team doesn't immediately respond healthily to a call for change, you might be ripe for an outside voice to help you arrive at a new place."[36]

Over the years several church planting directors asked me to consider coaching them. I hesitated, not thinking I had the time or the inclination to do this well. My friend, Brian Burman, who heads up coaching for Excel, suggested I put together a cohort for planting leaders. We tried it, and it has been helpful and encouraging to meet with leaders regularly to make sure we are getting back to the basics of the book of Acts.

Repeat

Real change comes with new habits being formed.

John Kotter, from Harvard Business School, emphasizes the need for short-term wins. Early, quick, positive successes give people who want to change a sense of new momentum: "Victories that nourish faith in the change effort, emotionally reward the hard workers, keep the critics at bay, and build momentum," Kotter adds, "without sufficient wins that are visible, timely, unambiguous, and

---

36   Carey Nieuwhof, *Lasting Impact: 7 Powerful Conversations That Will Help Your Church Grow* (The rethink Group, Inc., 2016).

meaningful to others, change efforts invariably run into serious problems."

Change occurs when we change our habits.

Reframe

Real change comes when we adopt a new perspective.

From a passenger ship, everyone can see a bearded man on a small island who is shouting and desperately waving his hands. "Who is that?" a passenger asks the captain. "I've no idea." The captain admits. "But every year when we pass, he goes nuts."

Maybe we'd be better off if we took another look, got another perspective, and framed things a bit differently.

We've tried to present a reframing of church planting from a Biblical perspective rather than the typical, cultural one in which we may be stuck.

Don't Give In

When our son, Tim, was maybe three or four years old, I came home from the office and asked Lori how her day went. She said it was kind of rough because she went to the park and Tim's bigger cousin knocked him off the swing, and he ended up on the ground crying. So I immediately took Tim off to his room, looked him in the eye and said, "If one of your cousins try to knock you off the swing, don't let them do it. Don't let them do it!" A few days later I came home and Lori said they had gone to the park with Tim's cousins again. I asked if there was another incident, and Lori said, "I didn't see what happened, but when I looked over, Tim was on the swing happily swinging away, while his cousin was on the ground crying." I looked over at Tim, and without saying a word he looked at me and simply smiled from ear to ear.

Tim learned a lesson we all may have been taught as kids: Don't let them do it! If we allow bullies to harass us, they will seize every opportunity to push us around. There is a time and place for boundaries, toughness, and simply saying, "Stop!" Don't give in to them.

We may have encountered that lesson at school, at work, or even at the park with our family members. But somehow we rarely allow that lesson into the church. Somehow we have thought letting others take advantage of us is "the Christian thing to do."

Of course Jesus taught us to turn the other cheek. But didn't he also demonstrate the need to turn the tables upside down when annoyance turns into exploitation?

There's another story from the book of Acts that hammers home the "Don't let them do it!" lesson:

> The next morning some Jews formed a conspiracy and bound themselves with an oath not to eat or drink until they had killed Paul. More than forty men were involved in this plot. They went to the chief priests and the elders and said, "We have taken a solemn oath not to eat anything until we have killed Paul. Now then, you and the Sanhedrin petition the commander to bring him before you on the pretext

Somehow we have thought letting others take advantage of us is "the Christian thing to do."

of wanting more accurate information about his
case. We are ready to kill him before he gets here."
—Acts 23:12-15 (NIV)

Paul had arrived in Jerusalem only to be arrested on
trumped-up charges. His accusers had taken matters to a
drastic place. They wanted him dead.

> But when the son of Paul's sister heard of this plot,
> he went into the barracks and told Paul. Then Paul
> called one of the centurions and said, "Take this
> young man to the commander; he has something to
> tell him." So he took him to the commander. The
> centurion said, "Paul, the prisoner, sent for me and
> asked me to bring this young man to you because
> he has something to tell you." The commander
> took the young man by the hand, drew him aside
> and asked, "What is it you want to tell me?" He
> said: "Some Jews have agreed to ask you to bring
> Paul before the Sanhedrin tomorrow on the pretext
> of wanting more accurate information about him.
> Don't give in to them, because more than forty of
> them are waiting in ambush for him. They have
> taken an oath not to eat or drink until they have
> killed him. They are ready now, waiting for your
> consent to their request."
> —Acts 23:16-21 (NIV)

Paul's nephew has a very clear message for the com-
mander, and for all of us:

Don't give in to them.

—Acts 23:21 (NIV)

They didn't give in:

> The commander dismissed the young man with this warning: "Don't tell anyone that you have reported this to me." Then he called two of his centurions and ordered them, "Get ready a detachment of two hundred soldiers, seventy horsemen and two hundred spearmen to go to Caesarea at nine tonight. Provide horses for Paul so that he may be taken safely to Governor Felix."
>
> —Acts 23:22-24 (NIV)

They refused to give in.

There is a time to turn the other cheek. This wasn't it. This was the time to say "No" to giving in to others.

When abuse is happening, don't give in to them. When others decline to listen to the Holy Spirit, don't give in to them. When the priorities get so messed up that the organization is put ahead of the gospel, don't give in to them. When we are told to protect rather than partner, don't give in to them. When they try to smash you into their one-size-fits-all box, don't give in to them. When others promote their kingdom over God's kingdom, don't give in to them. When they forbid you to plant in their town, don't give in to them. When they

When others promote their kingdom over God's kingdom, don't give in to them.

accidentally or overtly try to hinder church planting, don't give in to them.

Church planter Steve Sjogren blogged:

> If you are doing something outside the box, don't take your denomination's response overly seriously. If that's you, face it, chances are you will never be understood very well. In the midst of my success as a planter...I was more or less tolerated by the leaders of my denomination because I broke the mold of how they thought churches were supposed to be planted. Denominational leaders are linear, systems people who play by the book – the book they wrote. They don't know how to deal with innovators who are writing new books. They will admire your success, but they won't know what to do with your methods. It's best to just smile and flow with them as long as is possible. Don't be rebellious. Relish the wisdom they offer. Most of the time they are veterans who know their chops, but realize you are the one who is on site, not them. Don't be a knucklehead and reject their wisdom, but on the other hand, don't be an automaton and not weigh aspects of what they recommend.

Have you ever noticed the number of times in the book of Acts that the early church leaders replaced acquiescence with boldness? "No, we're not going to do that..." "Sorry, that's not going to stop us..."

These people are not drunk, as you suppose. It's only nine in the morning! No, this is what was spoken by the prophet Joel…

—Acts 2:15-16 (NIV)

Which is right in God's eyes: to listen to you, or to him? You be the judges! As for us, we cannot help speaking about what we have seen and heard.

—Acts 4:19-20 (NIV)

Now, Lord, consider their threats and enable your servants to speak your word with great boldness.

—Acts 4:29 (NIV)

Peter said to her, "How could you conspire to test the Spirit of the Lord? Listen! The feet of the men who buried your husband are at the door, and they will carry you out also." At that moment she fell down at his feet and died. Then the young men came in and, finding her dead, carried her out and buried her beside her husband.

—Acts 5:9-10 (NIV)

Peter and the other apostles replied: "We must obey God rather than human beings!"

—Acts 5:29 (NIV)

You stubborn people! You are heathen at heart and deaf to the truth.

—Acts 7:51 (NLT)

Peter answered: "May your money perish with you, because you thought you could buy the gift of God with money! You have no part or share in this ministry, because your heart is not right before God. Repent of this wickedness and pray to the Lord in the hope that he may forgive you for having such a thought in your heart. For I see that you are full of bitterness and captive to sin."

If we are going to change the church planting world, we are going to have to stop letting the status quo push us off a cliff.

—Acts 8:20-23 (NIV)

The list goes on and on.

I suspect they were just following the example of Jesus:

When they heard this, the people in the synagogue were furious. Jumping up, they mobbed him and forced him to the edge of the hill on which the town was built. They intended to push him over the cliff, but he passed right through the crowd and went on his way.

—Luke 4:28-29

Today might not be the time to let others run all over us.

If we are going to change the church planting world, we are going to have to stop letting the status quo push us off a cliff. If we are going to get unstuck, we are going to have to say something like: *"Stop!"*

Let's follow the example of Jesus, the example of the apostles, and let's heed the words of Paul's nephew: Don't give in to them.

THE KEY QUESTION:

Change or die?

THE BIG CHALLENGE:

Find a mentor who will help you develop new relationships, new habits and a new mindset regarding church planting.

CHAPTER 18

ALL THE WORLD'S A STAGE

I never knew how fulfilling and energizing setting someone else up for success in ministry could be. Then we started pouring into and supporting church planting pastors, and we got addicted. Kingdom thinking is transcendent thinking!

—Paul Mints

If we did all the things we are capable of doing we would literally astound ourselves.

—Thomas Edison

Do what you can, with what you have, where you are.

—Theodore Roosevelt

D aniel Nuñez couldn't shake the daunting thought. He sensed that God was calling him to start fifty churches in his hometown of Tijuana, Mexico. The vision kept popping up in Daniel's mind. So he decided to do something. He convinced his church to start a daughter church. It was a hit. So they planted another one, and another one, and another one...When I first met Daniel he had started fourteen, and was on the way to fifteen. We've had the privilege of partnering with Daniel over the past several years and last month number twenty-nine launched. I asked Daniel what that church's name was. He answered wryly, "Actually, it doesn't have a name, so we're calling it 'Number Twenty-Nine!'"

Some churches, like Daniel's, are excited about the possibilities and on board with reproducing. Others seem disinterested in church planting. Still others find themselves in the middle of those options.

In working with churches and pastors over the years, I've tweaked what some may have called "the stages of reproduction." Let's step through the stages:

The Stages
Resisting

Some churches are currently resisting reproduction. Like couples who have decided against having children, these churches do not want to reproduce. Church Planting expert Bob Logan uses the term "hostile" to describe how some pastors and churches respond to the idea of parenting a daughter church. One famous pastor of a mega-church in our country once remarked, "We came dangerously close to planting a daughter church."

Many churches are clearly on birth control.

Many churches are clearly on birth control.

Questioning

Other churches find themselves grappling with the clear Biblical command to "go forth and multiply." They are starting to wonder why this hasn't been part of the natural development in their church. They are asking questions, checking studies, and beginning to realize that they do not want to be, as multiplication specialist Red Ensley put it, "a dead-end link on the chain of Christianity."

Not Now, Maybe Later

Many churches, if not most, find themselves in the "Not Now, Maybe Later" stage. They realize that health leads to reproduction. They know that they need to parent someday. But they are caught up with other things right now. These folks typically say things like, "As soon as we get our facility built we'll consider a plant." Or, "We're not large enough yet." Or, "When we get our staffing, or program, or financial issues remedied, we'll look into it."

> **Some churches have had such a good experience in parenting, that they are having plenty of kids.**

Do Something

Some churches have moved to the place where they are actually doing something. They might be financially supporting a church planter or two. They may open their facilities to a church plant in their area or perhaps they've given gently-used equipment to a new church in the region. They have jumped into the game.

Aunt/Uncle

Other churches have moved to the point of being an Aunt or Uncle church. They might not feel ready to parent, but they are willing to generously support a planter. They're having planters come up front in their services, and are growing in support of a church planting movement.

God Parent

Some churches have moved a bit farther along the reproduction journey. They've become that special Aunt or Uncle – the God Parent. They are praying and giving and are available for special appeals by church plants for one-time gifts over and above previous commitments; they are available to send people to help out with a preview service; or to have a "baby shower" to buy items for a church plant's nursery. Our church in Elk Grove, Journey Church, has had this special relationship with a number of church plants across North America. We've told these churches to consider us to be a rich uncle who lives in California, and we try to slip them a few bucks every time we see them.

Parent

Some churches have actually moved to the point of "daughter-ing" a church. Like having kids biologically, this might be a deliberate, planned, thought-out strategy. A parent church might have the clear approach that they will give $50,000 to $100,000 and fifty to a hundred people to get a church launched. Or it might be more of "an accident." They might only be able to give a few bucks and a few people, but they are responding to God's personal call to be parents. They may or may not be joined by another parent church, but they've taken responsibility to help a church get going.

Baby Machine

Some churches have had such a good experience in parenting, that they are having plenty of kids. My four sisters have had seven kids, seven kids, six kids, and four kids respectively. And I've joked that they are baby-machines, constantly pregnant. Some churches are like that – they've become multiplication centers.

Wherever we are on the stages of reproduction, it would be wise if we took the next step...

Mini-Denomination

Ultimately, some have multiplied so much that they've approached becoming a denomination unto themselves. Their kids are having kids. Some are reproducing like wildfire, leaving a lasting legacy.

Churches range throughout these stages, from resistant to rapid reproduction.

The application is clear: let's identify where we, where our church (or organization) currently finds itself along the reproductive journey. Is your organization resistant? Questioning? Waiting? Involved? Moving toward parenting? Cranking them out?

Daniel Nuñez and I were in Cuba recently, and Daniel was telling his story – in Spanish – about his vision to plant fifty churches. As Daniel spoke, I overheard the young Cuban interpreter translate the vision as "fixty." He kept saying that Daniel wanted to plant fixty churches. So, later I mentioned to Daniel that he couldn't stop at only fifty churches, he needs to keep going! The real vision is for fixty!

Daniel said a few of his friends noticed a Spanish play on words: "Cincuenta Iglesias" means fifty churches. "Sin cuenta Iglesias" means churches without count!

Wherever we are on the stages of reproduction, it would be wise if we took the next step, kept going. Maybe we all can plant fixty churches, too – or maybe too many to even count!

THE KEY QUESTION:

Where are we on the stages of reproduction?

THE BIG CHALLENGE:

Move further along the reproductive line. If you're thinking, "Not now," I'd encourage you to rethink that and at least do something - support a church planter, give something. If you're doing something, consider taking on the challenge of being a God Parent. Or perhaps it is time to daughter that first church - or that second one. Let's move along the reproductive journey.

CHAPTER 19

THE HAND-OFF

How wonderful it is that nobody need wait a single moment to start improving the world.

—Anne Frank

Even if you're on the right track, you'll get run over if you just sit there.

—Will Rogers

Never put off till tomorrow what you can do the day after tomorrow.

—Mark Twain

A church planter familiar with our network included me in an email he sent out a few years ago. He was announcing that he was retiring and resigning immediately and moving to Southern California to become a pool man. I called the church's board chair, who explained their plans, "We're inviting people to stay after church this weekend so we can decide what to do...." That sounded sudden and scary, so I asked if I could attend, or send someone. They didn't want help. They swiftly decided to close the church down.

I didn't know the entire situation – this wasn't a church within our network, but closing a church is a last resort in my mind. To be honest, I threatened so many times over the years to quit the ministry and simply become a pool man that it became a sort of joke in our family. Maybe in this case, quitting had to be done, but there must be a better way to hand-off a ministry than to simply let it shut down.

Leadership Network once offered a webinar on "Succession!" It consisted of a couple dozen short videos by pastors and leaders who had transitioned out or transitioned in recently. Commonly used sentiments were, "My predecessor stayed too long, way too long…" "There was no plan…" and "It seemed like this was rougher than it had to be…" One son of a famous preacher recalled how his Dad never spoke of retirement or succession, then abruptly dropped dead. At the funeral everyone from the church was asking, "What do we do now?" He became the new leader by default.

> There must be a better way to hand-off a ministry than to simply let it shut down.

Bart Starr, the Hall of Fame quarterback, was once asked toward the end of his playing career, "What's the toughest play for an all-pro quarterback like you?" Starr didn't hesitate, he simply admitted, "The toughest play is the hand-off."

> Handing off a ministry is a play that is pretty much inevitable, yet we rarely talk about it.

A great way to start getting back to the book of Acts model of leadership reproduction is to start with ourselves by preparing for our own hand-off.

"May I take your order?" the waiter asked. "Yes, how do you prepare your chickens?" "Nothing special, sir," he replied. "We just tell them straight out that they're going to die."

Have you done anything to prepare for your hand-off, or to prepare for someone to hand off to?

Handing off a ministry is a play that is pretty much inevitable, yet we rarely talk about it. We think about it, we threaten to quit just about every Monday, but do we really have any idea how to do it?

> Paul and Barnabas chose some leaders for each of the
> churches. Then they went without eating and prayed
> that the Lord would take good care of these leaders.
> — Acts 14:23 (CEV)

> I left you in Crete to do what had been left undone
> and to appoint leaders for the churches in each town.
> —Titus 1:5 (CEV)

Paul and Barnabas worked on handing off their ministry. The Apostle Paul suggests that the hand-off is one of the plays Titus – and all of us – might need in our playbook. So what's the strategy? How do we do it?

How to Hand Off

I've been ruminating on this topic for some time now, and I certainly don't claim to have all the answers. But I do have a few tips. Here they are:

1. Realize it is not *your* ministry

> So guard yourselves and God's people. Feed and
> shepherd God's flock—his church, purchased with

his own blood—over which the Holy Spirit has
appointed you as leaders…

And now I entrust you to God and the message of
his grace that is able to build you up and give you an
inheritance with all those he has set apart for himself.
—Acts 20:28 & 32 (NIV)

We can get caught up thinking that our ministry is all
about us. But Paul calls that a rookie mistake. It isn't my
church, it isn't your ministry, it is God's. Paul most often
called it, "this ministry."

Therefore, since through God's mercy we have this
ministry, we do not lose heart.
—2 Corinthians 4:1 (NIV)

2. Take your influence and responsibility seriously

I originally labeled this point, "There's got to be a better way than we've been doing it…" Then I sarcastically
had it as, "The next time a search committee makes a good
decision will be the first time a search committee makes a good decision…"

We can get caught up thinking that our ministry is all about us.

Yes, I personally don't have great experiences with search committees. And I've
been hired by search committees. My first
encounter was with one in Denver that
hired me to do music. I don't play an instrument, I can't
sing very well, and I never learned to read notes, but other
than that I was their guy.

It seems like the typical search committee *means* well. They are trained over several months by capable leaders, then something happens – almost the entire team ends up resigning and a new team is formed. The church gets impatient and doesn't want to go through training again so they collect a huge stack of resumes. Unimpressed and overwhelmed, the committee is frustrated until some goodhearted member offers,

It seems like the typical search committee means well.

"Hey, my cousin-in-law from Cleveland is out of work, and he was a youth pastor a while back, why don't we go with him?" Then the committee decides quickly to hire the guy from Ohio and hope for the best.

Maybe I'm exaggerating. My Methodist friends don't seem to have it any better with their appointing system. They have a hundred churches, twenty-five gifted pastors, twenty-five unhealthy pastors who would probably drive any ministry into the ground within months, and a bunch in the middle. So they struggle with which churches to bless, and which churches can survive a lousy pastor for a while – and they go through it every year.

There's got to be a better way, right?

How about leadership?

> If anyone wants to provide leadership in the church, good!
> —1 Timothy 3:1 (MSG)

What if we kept leading until the hand-off was complete? I've handed off three church plants. The first one resulted in a fumble nine months after I left – yes, a gigantic search committee mistake that hobbled the church for a time. In the second hand-off, I stayed around and led, and the pastor who took over was voted in unanimously. He is still at that church – many, many years later (*and* he talked that California city into giving the church thirty-three acres of land!) The third hand-off was to my son, Tim. I didn't initiate that; our church leadership team did. We carefully did what we called, "The Switch!" Tim moved from Youth Pastor to Lead Pastor. I moved from Lead Pastor to Teaching Team Coach. We were meticulous with the details of the leadership shift, and it has worked out amazingly.

We don't have to bolt to the pool business immediately – we can stay and lead.

3. Begin with the end in mind

> For I am already being poured out like a drink offering, and the time for my departure is near. I have fought the good fight, I have finished the race, I have kept the faith.
>
> —2 Timothy 4:6-7 (NIV)

One day you will not be in your present position. One day you will retire, or die, or even become a pool cleaner. Why not start with that attitude?

Yes, we need to serve like we will be in this ministry forever, but we also need to plan like we may be pouring chlorine tomorrow.

4. Always be looking to develop leaders

> And the things you have heard me say in the presence of many witnesses entrust to reliable people who will also be qualified to teach others.
>
> —2 Timothy 2:2 (NIV)

Sure, Barnabas brought Saul into the Antioch church from the outside – "Tarsus" (Acts 11). But it seems like the normative hand-offs in the Book of Acts were from within the current ministry.

Sitting with my daughter, Tricia, and several of her teammates as they were getting ready to board a plane back to China at SFO a couple years ago, I overheard them planning on leadership succession for their present ministry. They were all going to be moving in less than a year and needed to find a leader for the hand-off. After a brief discussion they concluded that the next leader was probably going to be someone they hadn't met or led to the Lord yet. Wow!

> I suspect we all have better potential leaders in our midst than we give them credit for.

Every time I get a call or an email from a planter or pastor asking if "I know someone who might be interested in their worship, youth, or staff position...," my first – and silent – response is, "Raise up your own stinking leaders!"

I suspect we all have better potential leaders in our midst than we give them credit for.

5. Be patient

> You, however, know all about my teaching, my way
> of life, my purpose, faith, patience, love, endurance,
> persecutions, sufferings – what kinds of things hap-
> pened to me in Antioch, Iconium and Lystra, the
> persecutions I endured.
>
> —2 Timothy 4:10-11 (NIV)

Succession takes time.

6. Expect and embrace pain

> Join with me in suffering...
>
> —2 Timothy 2:3 (NIV)

Immediately after talking about reproduction, Paul talks about suffering. There is a correlation.

> When Paul had finished speaking, he knelt down
> with all of them and prayed. They all wept as they
> embraced him and kissed him. What grieved them
> most was his statement that they would never see
> his face again.
>
> —Acts 20:36-38 (NIV)

Pain puts the "sucks" in "succession!"

I think we're reluctant to plan and work and lead through this because it is so painful. It is not fun letting go; it is not pleasant training someone up, then having them flake out. It is hard work. Let's embrace the pain. Pool service is easier, but not eternal.

7. Get some help

> Do your best to come to me…
>
> —Titus 3:12(NIV)

> Do your best to come to me quickly…
>
> —2 Timothy 4:9 (NIV)

Timothy and Titus had help for their network. And there are experts who have been leading transitions for decades. Why are we not automatically letting them lead, and help us lead, through transitions?

I was sitting in a meeting talking about pastoral placement in a church when one of the experienced placement directors declared, "Against the strong recommendation of our network leaders the church has decided to bring two candidates in at the same time and have a sort of preach-off."

Most of the people in the room were stunned by the ridiculousness of that approach. But I was alarmed and amused by the opening phrase, "Against the strong recommendation of our network leaders…"

There are experts who have been leading transitions for decades. Why are we not automatically letting them lead through transitions?

Let's at least begin to work on our own hand-off.

THE KEY QUESTION:

Who will take the hand-off from you?

THE BIG CHALLENGE:

Identify your next step in preparing for your own hand-off.

CHAPTER TWENTY

SAY WHEN

A little less conversation, a little more action, please.

—Elvis Presley

I have been impressed with the urgency of doing. Knowing is not enough; we must apply. Being willing is not enough; we must do.

—Leonardo da Vinci

Vision is not enough. It must be combined with venture. It is not enough to stare up the steps, we must step up the stairs.

—Vaclav Havel

After waiting more than an hour and a half for her date, the young lady decided she had been stood up. She changed from her dinner dress into pajamas and slippers, fixed some popcorn, and resigned herself to an evening of TV. No sooner had she flopped down in front of the television than her doorbell rang. There stood her date. He took one look at her and gasped, "I'm two hours late . . . and you're still not ready?"

Are you ready? It is time to start changing…and stay changed!

An off-ramp of a freeway in Long Beach, California, has been torn up for years. Recently, someone put up a handmade sign reading, "Scientists tell us that the sun will burn out in one and a half billion years. It is sad that this contractor will have to finish working in the dark."

It is time to make something happen.

Bill Hybels, in his classic book, *Axiom,* tells this story in his chapter entitled, "The Bias Toward Action":

> I was helping a church with a building initiative a few years ago and on route from the airport to the church, the senior pastor and I talked about this 'bias toward action' concept. He told me that whenever he's considering hiring someone new, he gives the person a driving test. Are they looking for the faster lane? The shortest route? An edge on nearby drivers? We happened to be sitting at a stoplight while he was telling me all of this and somewhere mid-paragraph, the light changed from red to green. I waited a few seconds for him to notice, but no such luck. Finally, I couldn't choke it back: "It's as green as its gonna get, Mario. If you're so action-oriented, then step on it. I'm dying here!" Friend, it's as green as its gonna get in our world. The doors are open, the path is clear, the harvest is huge, and the time to act is now.[37]

Hybels adds,

> Personally, I've never understood inactivity. Why a person would sit when he could soar, spectate when he could play, or atrophy when he could develop

---

[37]   Bill Hybels, *Axiom* (Zondervan, 2008).

is beyond me. I'm sure Jesus felt the same way. A lot of adjectives might describe Jesus' time here on earth, but comatose would not be one of them. In the span of three years in "vocational' ministry," he performed dozens of miracles, healed hundreds of people, catalyzed thousands of conversions, set the stage for the most ambitious church plant in history, and died for the sins of all humankind. He was the epitome of action-orientation.[38]

Mae West declared, "You only live once, but if you do it right, once is enough."

It is time for us to make the most of the time we have been given.

My Dad had a saying, "It won't be long now...said the monkey as he backed into the lawnmower."

It is time to start.

Casey Stengel joked, "There comes a time in every man's life, and I've had plenty of them."

Well, now is the time.

> "Those who wait for perfect weather will never plant seeds; and those who look at every cloud will never reap a harvest."
>
> —Ecclesiastes 11:4

Napoleon Hill warned, "Do not wait; the time will never be 'just right'. Start where you stand, and work with

---

whatever tools you may have at your command, and better tools will be found as you go along."

And Zig Ziglar pronounced, "If you wait for all the lights to turn green before starting your journey, you'll never leave your driveway."

So start.

Start praying.

Pray for Holy Spirit encounters. Pray for wisdom. Pray for strength to change. Pray for the leaders already in your network. And pray for new leaders to emerge.

Start looking for leaders.

There just might be a Barnabas and Saul already in your midst. Pray for the eyes to see them, and then open your eyes!

Start giving toward church planting.

Maxey Jarman used to say, "Those who wait to give, rarely ever give." The light is as green as its going to get, Mario, so start sending funds in to church planting networks that are serious about changing the world.

Start requiring planters to ensure their new churches give generously.

We can make this a new part of our planting process immediately. Grandfather in existing planters if you must, but let's stop waiting to give.

Start partnering.

Start looking for like-minded leaders and networks who can help you change your church planting world.

Start moving away from being so concerned about our organization that we miss the leaders and the people in it.

Start allowing planters to plant wherever it is best to plant.

Even if it is right next door to an existing church. Allow it because it is the right thing to do.

Start using "Discovery" or "Discerning" rather than "Ass…" words.

You can start changing this today.

Start shaking off the shipwrecks.

Start celebrating reproducing churches even more than growing churches.

Any church that plants another church should be honored publicly and abundantly.

Andy Stanley encouraged, "Make a difference. Don't be satisfied with making a point."

Chandler Bolt put it well: "Done is better than perfect."

Start living intentionally.

Start something.

Michael Hyatt encourages, "Once you've determined your next step, take it. Don't wait."

A man walks into a restaurant wearing a shirt open at the collar. The bouncer meets him and announced, "I'm sorry. Gentlemen are not allowed into this establishment without a tie. So the man returns to his car to look for a necktie, but he doesn't have one. He sees a set of jumper cables in his trunk. In desperation he ties these around his neck, manages to fashion a fairly acceptable looking knot and lets the ends dangle free. He goes back to the restaurant and the bouncer carefully looks him over for a few minutes and then says, "Well, OK, I guess you can come in – just don't start anything."

> There just might be a Barnabas and Saul already in your midst. Pray for the eyes to see them, and then open your eyes!

We don't have to be that way. Let's start something. Let's take our energy and attach it to our leaders, churches, networks, denominations, and teams and lead the charge!

My son, Jake was driving me through congested downtown Atlanta traffic last summer when he shared, "Dad, one lesson you taught me well is, 'Sometimes a man's got to do what a man's got to do!' I was feeling pretty good about my parenting, until Jake added, "And Dad, you usually said that right before making an illegal U-turn." Then Jake made an illegal U-turn!

It doesn't have to be illegal, but let's make the U-turns we need to make. Let's lead the *other* way.

We can change the church planting world.

THE KEY QUESTION:

What is stopping me from taking some action right now?

THE BIG CHALLENGE:

Do something, just one thing to help change the church planting world today!

Acknowledgments

I have a ton of people to thank for helping this book become a reality.

My wife Lori has not only been my life partner, but also my church planting partner for over three decades. She is the number one person who helped make this book possible. Our kids: Tricia, Tim, Scott, Jake, Nicci, Sue, and Gionna have been a part of our church planting journey, and they gave input and encouragement every step of the writing process.

The Advisory Team of Excel Leadership Network deserves special kudos: David Bennett, Brian Burman, Geoff Wells, Luke Allen, Paul Mints, Karl Roth, Jeff Sharp, and Paul Taylor consistently supported this project.

Longtime assistants Rachel Kihlthau Taft, Sharon Wells, Tom Cullen, Kim Weaver, Veronica Becerra, Stephen Fussle, and Alan Adler freed me up to write.

The folks at Discovery Church and Journey Church in Elk Grove, California, warrant distinct gratitude. The Journey Teaching Team was incredibly helpful – especially Ben Finney who came up with most of the "Key Questions" and "Big Challenges." The ABC Team at

Journey: Tim, Geoff, Brad, Ben, and Scott were amazingly cooperative.

Excel's Consult Team: John Jackson, who said I needed to write this book; Dan Southerland, who graciously wrote the forward; Albert Tate, Mark Driscoll, and Adam Mabry proved to be very supportive.

I need to mention another writer, my brother, John Pearring, who encouraged and challenged me to make this happen.

Brett Burner served as editor, publisher, and writing coach. I am deeply indebted to Brett.

Willie Nolte, Jim Kennon, Doug Meye, Mike Pate, and the leaders at Transformation Ministries have been particularly encouraging.

And I would like to acknowledge the Launch Team for *Leading the Other Way*: Laurie Lang, Mike Pearring, Lindy Pearring, Lisa Pearring, Molly Pearring, Brian Harrington, Chris Hall, Scott Johnson, Eric Oleson, Aalim Bakari, Matt Van Peursem, Daniel Nunez, Cory Smithee, Aaron Clayton, Sean St. Clair, Robbie McLaughlin, Eric Beeman, Mike Pate, Chris Allen, Tommy Parke, Jay Nickless, Brad Brucker, Beto Pena, Bryon Scott, Brian Howard, Roy Tinklenberg, Chris Hansler, Alex Schweng, Richard Todd, Nathan Hawkins, Justin Davis, Andy Ziegenfuss, Eric Gamero, Ross Browning, Jared Kirk, Ace Sligar, Marlan Minks, Marlene Bertrand, BJ Johnson, Todd Hahn, Gordon West, Richard Reynolds, Dave Lodwig, Amy Mangili, Kory Tedrick, Bret Johnson, Peter Casillas, Brian Becker, Steve Dahl, Paul Root, Jason Wolfe, Joey Furjanic, Andrew Southwick, Micah Pelkey, Don Atkins, Tim Pettey,

ACKNOWLEDGMENTS

Adam Mabry, Nathan Couch, Brad Schottle, Scott Jones, Ben Finney, Kyle Hedwall, Dennis Beatty, Kevin Wood, Kennedy McGowan, Lance Whorton, Jarrid Wilson, John Helveston, Tom Nebel, Jack Francis, Stu Streeter, Bob Cherry, Chris Cassis, Joshua Meyer, Micah Foster, Joshua Meyer, Toby Carnes, Paul Nickerson, Rick Weber, Mike Wan, Roy and Wendy Clark, Mike Young, Vicki Kuyper, Jacob Lang, Nathan Hawkins, Andrew Alesso, John Pearson, Matt Golab, Jeff Sammons, Scott Wan, Waison Chen, Jerry Dahl, Edwin Collado, Bryan Hitch, Jack Igel, David Cobia, and Jeff Snodgrass.

CPSIA information can be obtained
at www.ICGtesting.com
Printed in the USA
FSOW02n1620270517
34721FS

9 781600 390258